How to Transform Your Ideas into Software Products

A step-by-step guide for validating your ideas and bringing them to life!

By Poornima Vijayashanker

Copyright

© 2014 by Poornima Vijayashanker.

Dedication

To everyone out there who has an idea, and
to those who support them in bringing that idea to life!

Acknowledgements

The following folks were kind enough to help me by reading through the early manuscript, providing feedback, and offering motivation to get me through the process:

Addison Huddy	Akshai Prakash
Ahmed Muzammil	Alyssa Ravasio
Adii Pienaar	Ben Congleton
Bernadette Cay	Blossom Woo
Brittany Forsyth	Carol Willing
Christian Russ	Christine Luc
David Acevedo	David Cummings
David Kadavy	Dave McClure
Dominic Jodoin	Fernando Garrido Vaz
Hiten Shah	Ilya Krasnov
Indi Young	Jason Pelker
James Russell	Jason van den Brand
Jocelyn Goldfein	John Siwicki
John Sawers	Julia Grace
Lauren Hasson	Lonnie Kragel
Marina Braverman	Melody McCloskey
Mila Vukojevic	Noah Kagan
Renata Lima	Ritika Puri
Sramana Mitra	Silvie Hibdon
Tamara Austin	Tim Kent
Thomson Nguyen	Zakiullah Khan Mohammed

Thank you for all your time and efforts in getting this book out of my head and into print :)

I'd also like to thank our kind sponsors for making it possible to create a print version of this book: Framed Data, Hackbright, New Relic, and Shopify.

Special thanks to: Nathan Barry for educating me and helping me navigate the self-publishing process; Nathalie Arbel, my encouraging and thoughtful editor, who kept up with me and helped me stay true to my voice; my designer, Shiran Sanjeewa, who took on the project at a moment's notice; and my assistant, Justin Reyes, for everything you do every day!

You've all contributed immensely to this project, and I'm happy it bears your mark on it.

A final thank you to my dear boyfriend, Aaron Wilson, who was there to help me keep my chin up and my belly full!

Table of Contents

Introduction

When I was growing up, my dad would come home from work and say things like, *"I've spent the whole day packaging up chips."* Or, *"Those wafers have a lot of defects in them."* Meanwhile, I'd be thinking, *Yummy... my dad makes potato chips and vanilla wafers!* And I always wondered why he never brought any home.

One fateful day, my dad came home and asked me if I'd like to visit a **fab**, or fabrication facility, where he worked. Of course, I said yes, and I was really excited!

The next day as we approached the fab my dad warned me not to touch anything because the oils from my hands would contaminate the chips and wafers. I agreed that I wouldn't. As I walked into the facility I noticed that people were decked out head to toe in white outfits (I later learned these were called "bunny suits"). I kept a lookout for anything that resembled a snack.

But the only thing I spotted that was interesting to me was a small glass box in the middle of the room. As I approached the box, I noticed that a tiny robotic arm was very precisely picking up one small black square at a time and moving it to another side.

In that moment, I completely forgot about the reason I was there and became mesmerized by the precision of this robotic arm.

At that point, my dad explained that he was a hardware engineer, and he made *silicon* wafers and *microchips* that went into computers. Oh! I wasn't disappointed—rather, I became more intrigued by technology.

I wanted to combine my years of research, lessons, and collaboration with real-life entrepreneurs into an easy-to-follow guide. This book begins by helping you choose the right idea and then lays out a roadmap for launching and sustaining it as a profitable business. If you stick with me through the whole journey, we will transform your brainchild from rough sketch to useful software!

To create a successful product in any industry, you first have to make sure your idea is valid.

What is idea validation?

It's the process of:

1. Sharing an idea with others, getting constructive feedback, and parsing responses to find common themes.

2. Identifying actual problems people are experiencing in the world, versus what you believe or guess are problems, then designing a solution to address these issues.

3. Figuring out who is experiencing the problem and whether your solution will solve it for them.

4. Making sure those who want your solution will also value it by paying for it.

5. Looking ahead at the potential product's context and market to determine whether the idea could eventually become a viable business.

Why should idea validation happen early?

An idea doesn't equal a product, and having a product doesn't mean people will want it!

Having built software for the past 10 years in Silicon Valley, I've noticed that most people who want to build software products take the trial-and-error approach, and I've met countless people who come up with an idea and jump right into building it.

The results are almost always the same. It's unclear:

- whom the product is for;
- what the benefits are; and
- whether it's actually worth anything.

The product gets low signup rates, and often the people who do sign up are unwilling to pay for it.

Eventually, this leads the creators of the product to lose sight of their original vision, lose motivation, and wind up regretting their decision to create a product in the first place. They've spent countless hours, weeks, months, and maybe even years on this idea, and have invested resources and energy into it. They learn the hard way that a trial-and-error approach is time consuming and expensive, and they could have avoided this by taking time upfront to validate their ideas.

When you validate early, you also increase the chance that you can raise capital from angel investors and VCs. These days, that is what it takes to strike their fancy. Most want to see that you've at least built a prototype, attracted customers, and generated some revenue.

The first few chapters of this book will show you how to identify an idea you believe in and then validate it before spending too much effort.

The lean startup methodology popularized this approach, but it doesn't just apply to startup companies; I've seen its applications at large enterprises and nonprofits. Similarly, idea validation and many other techniques in this book apply to a wide variety of products: software, hardware, informational products, and physical goods. As someone who has built all of them, I know there is overlap. However, this guide focuses on building software products.

Why software?

Since its inception, software has played a major role in high tech. Its most popular applications are to:

Compute.

Software's initial intent was to improve computational efficiency. Whatever took humans hours, weeks, months, or years to do, computers could do faster! The sophistication and size of data sets has advanced over the years, creating a new category called big data, and software helps us benefit.

Connect.

Software has been connecting individuals across the world for decades, but the rise of social networks, search engines, and marketplaces has made us grow even closer, strengthening relationships and making online commerce possible.

Automate.

In the late '90s, people started to use software to automate repetitive and rote tasks, but this was limited to the enterprise market. In the past decade, creating applications for consumers has become easier and even cost effective, leading to even more productivity gains.

Entertain.

Who doesn't love watching a cat on a roomba? Thanks to the advent of video platforms like YouTube and blogging sites, user-generated content keeps us entertained and engaged for hours!

Fortunately, over the years it's become easier to develop and deploy applications that benefit billions of people around the world. Software creation has come very far since my first encounter with the fab. In my first computer science course, my professor talked about how he used to program on punch cards back in the '70s. They were cumbersome to program on: one minor bug, and he'd have to wait almost a whole day for a machine to be available so he could fix it!

Listening to his stories and the stories of other professors gave me a sense of how far the industry had come by improving software development and making it easier to create applications. Much of this is thanks to:

Distribution.

As late as 2005, if people wanted to develop their own software applications and distribute them to people around the world, they had two options. The first was to burn it to a CD, shrink wrap it, and then sell it through a retail vendor like Best Buy or CompUSA. The second was to leverage the Internet and buy a server that would host the application. Both of these methods were cumbersome and costly. However, thanks to the advent of managed hosting services like Amazon, EngineYard, Heroku, Rackspace, and others, people can focus on building their applications and then quickly and easily deploy them to a third-party server that will handle the distribution.

Tools, languages, and frameworks.

Developer productivity has gone through the roof. I remember my college days when I'd have to spend 10 minutes compiling my code, only to discover that I had a compiler error! Fortunately, now there are a lot of great frameworks such as Ruby on Rails, Django for Python, and even dynamic typed languages like JavaScript that let you quickly code and see what you've made. Other tools like Github have made it easier to track and manage source code.

Process improvements.

More people are adopting practices like Agile coupled with continuous integration and continuous deployment techniques. This has enabled them to move away from building big and bulky feature sets. Instead, they can write code, release it whenever they want, and receive feedback faster from customers too!

While it's easier than ever to develop software applications today, the plethora of products in the market has made the space highly competitive. Successfully building and bringing applications to market takes serious forethought. There are several related myths about software products that I think are worth debunking. The following two are the most common.

Myth 1: Software is easy to build.

Compared to physical products, software is faster to build because the iteration cycles go by quickly. But that doesn't necessarily mean it's easy. Designing a software product and maintaining it still takes a significant amount of time and expertise.

Myth 2: Software is inexpensive to build.

It's inexpensive to distribute, which is why it's such a high-margin business compared to physical products that require you to pay for shelf space. But last time I checked, software engineers' salaries were pretty much on the rise, both inside and outside of Silicon Valley. Even outsourcing has gone up in price!

In addition to the expenses of building software products, you'll need to think about attracting customers, which also costs money.

Therefore, early-stage idea validation and prudent business planning are crucial to save time and cash. This book will guide you through them step-by-step.

Will this guide work?

I've built products using these exact techniques and have taught my process to hundreds of people—both technical and non-technical—around the world. They've gone on to build software that people love and pay for. I did this through my own company, Femgineer, where I've taught 6 iterations of my Lean Product Development Course[1], including one at Duke University's Pratt School of Engineering in the fall of 2013. Most recently, I was invited to be an EIR (entrepreneur-in-residence) at 500 Startups[2], an accelerator based in Silicon Valley.

I've also researched and interviewed other prominent innovators, and have included much of their experience and best practices in the interviews in this guide.

On the other hand, I know everyone out there talks about what they did to succeed, but hardly anyone talks about what didn't work, and why. Failure isn't a bad thing. It helps us learn, because it forces us to take the time to step back, analyze, and understand what isn't working and think about what we could do better. I want you to learn from my failed experiments and experiences as well as those of others, so I've included a number of those stories in this guide.

If you stick with me, follow the steps I've outlined in this guide, and put them into practice with the exercises in each chapter, then you'll also be able to build products that people will love and pay for!

Who is this book for?

I've designed this guide with the following people in mind:

Technical folks

such as developers, designers, engineers, and product managers. They may be consultants, freelancers, employed by startups, or large companies. Their goals may be to stop trading hours for money by creating a product for themselves, or to create a product within a larger organization.

Entrepreneurs

who have an idea for a startup and want to cut to the chase by quickly validating the idea and bringing it to market.

This guide is also for those who struggle with:

- coming up with ideas;
- having too many ideas;
- knowing whether their idea is the right one; or
- knowing the steps to take when productizing an idea.

Who this guide isn't for:

If you're looking to learn how to code, then you'll be thoroughly disappointed. There isn't a single line of code in this guide. I do offer some best practices when it comes to development; however, the focus is to teach you how to validate your idea and then either build it yourself or recruit a team to build it for you.

If you're looking for a get-rich-quick scheme, this guide isn't for you either. The steps in this book will put you on a fast track to bringing your product to life, but you still have to do the exercises included in order to reap the benefits, which will take some time. How *much* time depends on your level of productivity. It also comes down to how the market responds to your product. If you're trying to build something for a very niche segment, then chances are it will take time to find and attract a base of early adopters who understand your product's benefits.

How this guide is organized, and how to use it:

I've ordered the chapters based on a process that I follow when productizing an idea. The book begins with idea validation exercises. Then, it provides a roadmap to clarify how to bring your validated idea to life and turn it into a profitable business. We'll touch on how to build a prototype, attract customers, measure success, get funding, manage a team, and more.

Even if you're far along in your product-creation journey, I highly recommend reading each chapter, because you might discover strategies you hadn't known about before. Each one is backed up by examples and case studies from my own experiences as well as exclusive interviews with startup founders and early employees from companies like Pardot, Tindie, Olark, and more.

I highly recommend treating this guide like you would treat a cookbook. If you've cooked anything before, you know that missing an ingredient or skipping a step in a recipe can affect the dish in the end! The exercises I've provided in this book are like recipes. Each one lays out steps and suggests tools to use.

You can find more resources, links, and tutorials by visiting this guide's website: *http://femgineer.com/transform-ideas*.

Transforming an idea takes time and hard work, but know that it's indeed possible and you can make it happen. So, let's get started!

Chapter 1

How to Come Up with Ideas, Pare Them Down, and Share Them!

I don't have an idea...

Over the years, I've met a lot of folks who struggle with generating ideas. What I've discovered during my conversations with them is that they do indeed have ideas, and in fact, generating them comes naturally! The reason they think they don't have ideas is because they're judging each of them too harshly, thinking that it just isn't good enough!

If you're struggling to come up with ideas, ask yourself if it's because you've told yourself, "*Oh that's already been done!*" Or "*Who would want something like that?*"

If yes, I have some news for you: ALL ideas suck initially! There is a process of refinement that takes place. However, to refine an idea and turn it into a product that people will love, you have to start by putting your judgment aside.

I also hear from people who tell me that they have an idea, but they're just not sure they love it.

Being personally interested in an idea is important. It's what will motivate you to jump out of bed in the morning to work on it. However, I also recommend that people don't fall in love with an idea but instead fall in love with the process of refining it and building it.

This is because as you start to refine your idea, you might find that it changes dramatically from what you started with. At that point, it's up to you to decide if you want to pursue this new path or give up altogether because you've strayed from the original idea you loved so much.

Many successful products drastically deviated from their original ideas, but in doing so, found loving customer bases.

Exercise 1.1: Get unstuck!

Objective: Introduce you to some techniques for idea generation.

Directions: Go through each of these techniques and use it to generate an idea. If you already have an idea, then you can skip ahead to the next exercise.

1. **Scratch your own itch.** You might have had a problem in the past that you created a solution for. Write it down. The next step is to figure out whether there are more folks like you who need this solution—I'll cover how to do that next.

2. **Refine an existing product.** There are a lot of software products today that need to be overhauled! Think of the products out there that are still shrink-wrapped software solutions, might be really hard to use, or are only catering to a subset of a market. Write down the products you think you'd like to refine.

3. **Look for a new problem.** There may be new problems that have emerged and don't yet have solutions. Can you think of any? Write them down.

4. **Start with a new technology or a new medium (mobile, Internet of Things, etc.) and create an application for it.** What are some new technologies you're familiar with? Can you think of an application for it? Write it down.

5. **Transform a service into a product.** If you're a freelancer or consultant you've probably seen some common themes in what your clients want. If you're tired of trading hours for money, then think about productizing your service offerings. In doing so, you'll also be able to service a larger base of users. I'll describe how to do this in the chapter on

"Getting Working Capital." For now, write down the services you think you could productize.

Section 2

I have too many ideas...

What a great problem to have! I'm a firm believer in focus, but I know that's hard, so you won't hear me telling you to pick one and then execute.

Instead, I'm going to tell you to run through the exercises in this book on all of them. Yup, that's right–all of them! If you do, then one of the following things will happen:

- You'll come to the realization that there just aren't enough hours in your day to run experiments on all your ideas and decide to put some on the back burner.

- You'll see results for one of them that are promising and then choose to focus on that one.

- You may notice a common theme emerge as you experiment, then integrate all your ideas into one!

Section 3

Is this the right idea?

Just like the folks who struggle with generating ideas, you might also be judging your idea too harshly. You'll have to learn to judge less, and instead, run experiments on your idea to test its validity.

Exercise 1.2: Introspect and contemplate your idea.

Objective: Make sure you understand why you are pursuing this idea.

Directions: Write down answers to each of the following questions.

1. **Why is this idea important to you?** Was it based on a personal experience? Do you have some specific domain expertise? If the idea isn't important to you, then it will never be the right idea.

2. **Who is the idea for?** Is this a group that resonates with you personally, so you want to help them out? If you don't have a level of empathy, then once again, it won't be the *right* idea.

Ultimately, judging if an idea is the right idea is based on a balance of the following:

- You personally love it and are OK with the process of refining it.

- You have a vested interest in improving the lives of the people with whom you are sharing it: your customers.

- Your conscience is clear about how it benefits people and how you make money from selling it.

Section 4

Consider working on someone else's idea first

When I was 6, my friend and I decided that we wanted to be millionaires and be able to pay for college—call us precocious, or maybe a little bit clairvoyant (we knew that the cost of college was going up). We decided that to make money, we'd make the only thing we knew how to make: popcorn balls.

We also figured that we had to go local before we could go global! So we started by walking door-to-door to sell our popcorn balls.

Guess how many popcorn balls we sold after one week?

ZERO!

Given that I was six at the time, I lacked a few entrepreneurial traits like vision, determination, and discipline.

After a week, I decided that being an entrepreneur was not in the cards for me, and I went back to doing what I knew I was good at: fixing electronic stuff around the house.

Fast forward to 2004. I arrived in Silicon Valley and took my first job as an R&D engineer. While I was curious about startups and building products, I figured I would need a lot of experience to bring an idea to life.

About a year later, my buddy from college, Aaron Patzer, gave me a call and told me about his idea for a startup. He said he was frustrated with personal finance software. All existing solutions were too complicated and took a long time to set up and manage. He wanted to create something that was simple for young people who were conscious of their finances but didn't want to spend a whole lot of time managing them. His vision was to create a simple software solution that enabled you to simply log in and see all your finances at once.

I thought this was a great idea!

On a ski trip to Tahoe we got stuck in a snowstorm and he started to talk to me about his idea. I asked him what he was going to call it. And he responded with *"Money Intelligence."*

"Money Intelligence?!" I thought it was a super-lame name and wouldn't attract young people, and I told him so. He challenged me to come up with something better.

I thought for a minute and replied, *"How about Mint?"* Aaron instantly grinned and said he loved it.

From that moment on, I was thrilled to have made a contribution and really wanted to start working on Mint.com with Aaron.

About 9 months later, I joined the team as the founding engineer. During the 3½ years I was at Mint.com, I learned a lot. I learned how to build a prototype, launch it, scale it, keep it secure, and attract customers. This was more than I expected.

After the acquisition, I was at a crossroads, unsure of what I wanted to do next.

I remembered how much I had sucked as a 6-year-old entrepreneur, but now I was 27; I had learned a lot over the years and decided that it was time to go from being an engineer to an entrepreneur.

You might feel the same way I did: unsure if you can really strike out on your own. It's only natural to have some self-doubt.

If you're not sure, then I'd encourage you to get started by working on someone else's idea. You can still apply all the strategies from this guide to that idea!

If you're looking for ways to connect and contribute to other people's ideas, here are a few resources I'd recommend:

- **CodeMontage**: You can find open source projects for social good on this site and make any size contribution, large or small.[3]

- **Startup Weekend**: Depending on where you live, there may be one coming to your city soon. It's a great place to gather with like-minded individuals who are looking to bring their ideas to life.[4]

Section 5

Fearing thought crime

In case you're wondering what **thought crime** is, it's the fear that someone will steal your idea, run off with it, and build it, leaving you in the dust! To combat it, you stay in "stealth mode," make people sign non-disclosure agreements (NDAs), or just don't share the idea until the product has launched.

Here's the truth, and I'm only going to say this once: if your idea is any good, eventually someone *will* steal it. So let's hope it's a good one!

The most common thieves are competitors, and on occasion, a previous employee.

The key is to be in the lead and have the expertise that they don't have!

You probably already have the expertise if the idea is based on a problem you've experienced yourself. The next step is to be in the lead, and to do that, you've gotta get comfortable sharing your idea.

Why?

Because while you may think your idea is amazing, and it probably is, it can always be made better! Making it better means getting feedback from others, including potential teammates, customers, and investors.

You can try to make them sign an NDA, but many people are reluctant to do so, because they might be seeing a LOT of different ideas daily. It's hard for them to remember which is which and to keep their lips sealed.

If you feel like you have some really top-secret sauce, like a patent pending technology, then just don't talk about it! It's easier to do that than to take someone to court and fight an NDA breach.

Figure out a way to share the overall theme of your idea in a way that a layperson can understand and provide you with feedback.

Now you might still think this is a whole lotta humbug. If you still don't believe me, then I'll challenge you to come up with an idea and tell it to the world! Even give your competitor a call and tell them. Chances are they won't have the bandwidth to do what you're doing, or they may be going in a different direction so they just won't care.

It is really hard for someone—even a large competitor—to reproduce your exact idea. Most competitors are going to wait until you have something proven, and then they'll use all their resources to copy it! But then they're not innovating—you are, and you'll be leading them.

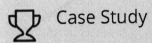

Case Study

Why we didn't fear thought crime or competition at Mint.com

When I was at Mint.com, our competitor, Intuit, had a much bigger team and lots of resources. A year after we launched, they saw our growth and thought that they could just copy us. They offered a product similar to ours called Quicken Online. They even offered it for free. Ultimately, hardly anyone used Quicken Online. People thought the product was complicated, even though it was free. We were in the lead, and it was hard for them to copy our ease-of-use and attract a similar group of users!

Hopefully, by this point you've been persuaded to share your idea. But if you're still not convinced, then I'm going to give it one last stab.

If you hold on to your idea, build it into a product, and then launch it without setting up a process to take in ongoing feedback for refinement, then you're going to have a pretty quiet launch day.

Why?

Because you've built a product based on one person's needs and opinions: yours. While you may think many people suffer from this problem, you are more biased than you think. If you are building a product that you want others to use, then you need to be taking feedback in *constantly*.

When I say constantly, I mean daily, weekly, and monthly!

This does not mean you have to react to every piece of feedback you receive, but it does mean that you need to be asking for it and collecting it in order to refine your idea. I'll talk about how to distill feedback in a future lesson. For now, collect away!

Hopefully, I've convinced you by now that you need to share your idea. Let's move on and talk about how to do this.

Section 6

Formula for sharing your idea

Here's the thing: a lot of people won't get your idea initially or be interested at all. Don't take this the wrong way, because I've been guilty of doing this too, but you might be presenting your idea in a complicated manner. The formula you want to go for is the following:

state whom the solution is for
+
state problem
+
state solution
+
the benefit

The order matters! You always want to start with the person who will benefit from your idea and the problem, because it elicits an emotional response. The same thing happens when you end with the benefit—you get a positive emotional response.

Here's a simple example:

If you are budget-conscious person who doesn't want to spend hours managing your money then you'll want a solution like Mint.com. Mint.com is an online personal finance website that lets you get a complete picture of your finances within minutes with no data entry. Using Mint will help you save time and grow your money!

Notice that I don't talk about the features. I start by mentioning whom the product is for: someone who is budget-conscious, so if you're rolling in the dough it's NOT for you. I talk about the problem: managing money is time consuming. I mention the name of the solution: Mint.com. Finally, I state the benefits: *save time and grow your money.*

You want to be clear about who is going to benefit from your solution. Too often, people fall into the trap of making their ideas too general. "Whom you're building a product for" is known as a user segment. If you're not sure who your initial user segment is, then you can test your product out on multiple groups. When I was getting started with my second startup, BizeeBee, my user segments were yoga studio owners and private instructors.

While you want to eventually build for multiple user segments, you should initially begin with one to two well-defined user segments.

Why does this matter? And why can't you go broad to begin with?

Because you're just getting started! It is very hard to build something that will appeal to everyone from day one. Believe me, I know!

Case Study

Why I narrowed our user segment at BizeeBee

While my startup, BizeeBee, services yoga studios and private yoga instructors today, I began by trying to appeal to all small businesses—a very general user segment.

When we launched the beta version of BizeeBee back in August 2010, we marketed it to all small businesses as a cash flow management tool. We got a lot of signups on day one, because a lot of small businesses struggle with managing their cash flow. But on day two, no one returned to use the product. At the two-week mark, after not seeing any users return, I got worried and started to call them up.

Turns out our product wasn't meeting the needs of the small businesses that offered products, had multiple locations, or were consultants who sold their time! Even though we thought we had limited our user segment, it was still too broad. That's when I knew I needed to hone in on a segment even further, so I chose to focus on fitness businesses. Over the years, we've honed it even further, servicing small independent fitness businesses (usually sole proprietorships). About 80% of our businesses are yoga studios.

Exercise 1.3: Create an idea summary and sl

Objective: Get comfortable using the followi.

> state whom the solution is for
> +
> state problem
> +
> state solution
> +
> the benefit

You will share this idea summary and hone it based on the feedback you get.

Directions: When you are requesting feedback, be as specific as possible! Being too open-ended in initial conversations can lead to few responses.

I know you want people to give you open-ended feedback, but honestly, people are time starved and have limited attention spans. So if you want something from them, you just have to be direct.

Start with a question like *"Is the idea clear? (Please give a yes or no response.)"*

People are great at giving yes or no responses. You can progress from there to *"If it wasn't clear, what wasn't clear about it?"* Even in this case, fill in the gaps with things like, *"Was it the wording, the design...?"*

Now, there may be those who are willing to give more feedback, so to prompt them with a final question, ask, *"Is there anything else you'd like to add or remove?"*

I guarantee you, if you present your idea using this formula to request feedback, two things will happen:

...ple will immediately understand it and WANT it.

People will immediately understand it and NOT want it. (This is a good thing, and I'll explain why shortly!)

If you get any other response, like, "*Hmm, does it do this...?*" then they're wrapping their head around the idea and you can just make a note of it for now.

I know this feels a little hand-wavy right now, but my goal is to get you comfortable sharing your idea and soliciting feedback. Don't read into good or bad responses too much at this point, because we're just getting started. For now, just note the responses.

Section 7

Early adopters are a special breed of customer

Let's assume you get one of the two above responses. Here's where things get interesting. For the group that wants it, consider those your early adopters. Early adopters are what we're after because they are in desperate need of your idea and want to experience the benefits you talk about. They will not care that it isn't perfect or doesn't have XYZ feature. They are willing to take a risk.

For the group that doesn't want it, it's still important to build rapport with them. Dig into what their concerns are, but do NOT try to convince them of your idea. Just realize that they may be willing to use it in the future, but not right now. Keep them updated about your progress; they may join in a year or two from now.

Let's tie this into the above exercise. If you did it, you might have received some negative feedback, which is actually a good thing! It might not seem like it because you're probably thinking, "*Sigh* my product sucks," or "*Ugh, what do they know!*"

Here's why receiving negative feedback is a good thing: it means you got your idea across! The person giving the feedback said that they weren't interested in it because it wasn't built yet, it was missing XYZ feature, or they just weren't sure. These people are NOT early adopters. They are mainstream folks who need a lot of validation. They want to hear from their friends and family about your idea. They want others to take a chance on it. They do not want take a risk.

While it's important to acknowledge the feedback of mainstream customers, you don't want to focus on them initially because you'll end up spending way too much time trying to please them. Even if you build exactly what they want, they will question your credibility! They fear startups and young products that might go under.

The key is to focus on finding your early adopters, and I'll dig into how to do that in Chapter 4. Another benefit to focusing on early adopters is that they will become your evangelists. They will fall in love with your product and go out and tell mainstream customers about it. Word-of-mouth marketing is the most powerful tool out there.

Think about the last time you purchased a product. Did you just go out and take a chance on something new or did you hear about it from a friend or family member? If it was the former, then you're an early adopter. If it's the latter, then you're a mainstream customer and you needed word-of-mouth marketing to convince you.

If you haven't gotten a group of early adopters yet, we'll talk about how to get them in Chapter 4.

 Review

If you are struggling with generating ideas, perhaps you're just judging them too harshly. If you truly are having difficulty coming up with them, then follow the steps I've laid out in Exercise 1 and write out your responses. Then dig a little deeper and ask yourself why the idea is important to you and whom it is for.

If you're still stuck but want to build a product no matter what, consider working on someone else's idea first.

You'll need to learn to get comfortable sharing your idea and soliciting feedback if you're serious about productizing it. Don't be too dismayed by any negative feedback you receive right now; it's more important to just get the feedback. Finally, remember that we're just getting started!

Interview with Melody McCloskey, CEO and Co-founder of StyleSeat

StyleSeat[5] launched in 2011 and is on a mission to help the world look and feel amazing by connecting anyone with the beauty services they need at any time. They help beauty and wellness professionals in over 15,000 cities across the US manage and grow their businesses through their online and mobile platforms. StyleSeat has raised $14.9M in capital from angels and venture capitalists and is headquartered in San Francisco, CA.

As you read my interview with Melody, you'll learn how as a non-technical founder she wasn't deterred from starting a technology company. She was able to build a prototype without a technical co-founder, and eventually recruited one: Dan Levine.

You'll also learn from Melody that it pays to focus on building a product for a niche market, and you'll hear about how she raised capital from angels and venture capitalists to scale her company.

Poornima: "Hi Melody, I appreciate you sharing your time and background with our readers! Let's start with your background. What was your major in college?"

Melody: "I went to UC Davis and majored in International Relations and French."

Poornima: "Did you have any experience programming?"

Melody: "In high school, I took AP C++ and dropped out of it. I was the only girl in the class, and I didn't want to get a C! I do regret dropping it."

Poornima: "So how did you get into tech then?"

Melody: "I first got into tech because most of my friends were engineers and founders. After college, I was told to pursue PR [public relations] because that's what women do. But I was the worst person on the planet for it. Then I went on to work at Seagate and startups. Soon I realized that it was an industry that I was obsessed with."

Poornima: "And why did you decide to become a founder?"

Melody: "I worked at a startup as a product manager, and that taught me how to communicate with engineers and designers. But it took me a couple years to feel like I could start a company myself. I thought only engineers started companies. I saw that things were changing."

Poornima: "How did you come up with the idea for StyleSeat?"

Melody: "I've always been into style, and I was looking for someone who was good and tried using Yelp. But after having 3 haircuts and colors, I was not happy. Then I went to someone who was amazing, and I felt really good. And I thought, *'How can I give this feeling to everyone else? How can I give them that experience?'* It's not a vanity thing, it's allowing you to be your best self."

Poornima: "Since you mentioned you're not technical, how did you build the prototype?"

Melody: "I loved all the details around building, and I knew how to manage a developer. I worked closely with a developer and cobbled together an initial solution."

Poornima: "What was in the prototype?"

Melody: "It was a client tracking tool. Independent stylists love using pen and paper. It's the only way they can keep track of their clients. The big salons have software, but if an employee wants to leave, they can't easily take their clients with them."

Poornima: "Was Dan Levine the initial developer?"

Melody: "No, I recruited Dan later. Because I had cobbled together a solution, he saw the vision of what I wanted to build."

Poornima: "Most people would think that this is a niche market. How did you convince investors it wasn't?"

Melody: "I did market research and found out that beauty is a $78B industry in the US and $130B globally."

Poornima: "Was that enough to convince them?"

Melody: "We also showed metrics over time. And while traction and product will speak for themselves, building relationships also has value. I had to build relationships with investors."

Poornima: "How did the product and vision change over time?"

Melody: "We began building a client tracking application and added scheduling, then in 2013 we focused on online booking and being a directory."

Poornima: "It's hard to have a big vision and deal with the day-to-day. How did you reconcile having a big vision with hitting your milestones?"

Melody: "We had major milestones and mini-milestones. My co-founder Dan complements me because he is very bottoms-up and focuses on what we need to build next."

Poornima: "What keeps you motivated and moving past rejection?"

Melody: "One of my really good mentors, Travis Kalanick, taught me that no one is as smart about your business as you. You know your customer. You've done the research. It's a combination of trusting your instinct and gut. Having your act together, knowing the numbers and data. But there will be naysayers. People who don't get it, because they don't know. You have to help people feel as passionate about it as you do. You have to say: '*let me tell you about the opportunity.*'"

Poornima: "What is one piece of advice you'd give to those starting out?"

Melody: "Find the smartest person you can find who has already been through it and can help. I found a female entrepreneur who helped close partnerships. Now I have Justin Caldbeck, who sits on my board and helps me build an executive team. You need to find good true partners: people with time who have done it before."

Poornima: "Thank you, Melody!"

 Just to recap, here's what we learned from Melody McCloskey:

1. **You don't need to be technical,** but you do need to know how to communicate with developers and convey your vision to them.

2. **If you're thinking about fundraising,** you'll need to have data, show results over time, and develop deep relationships with investors.

3. **When dealing with naysayers,** you need to educate those who don't grasp your idea on an emotional level, communicate the opportunity, and make them understand your passion.

 Chapter 2

Start with a Side Project

Back when I was working on Mint.com in 2007, I wanted another creative outlet to share my thoughts and experiences on engineering and entrepreneurship.

I decided to start a blog called Femgineer[6]. But before I could actually start blogging, there were a number of setup steps I had to complete, including buying a domain name, getting hosting, setting up a website, and designing the blog. After all that, I could finally sit down to blog!

Initially, blogging meant just chronicling my experiences. I didn't think anyone was actually reading my blog, but I knew there were a handful of people who actually subscribed to it. About a year later, as I went to conferences and networking events, people would recognize me from my blog! They'd talk about my posts and ask me to go into more detail. That's when I realized that I had an audience, and that I needed to be taking this whole blogging thing a little more seriously.

From that point on, I put more effort into coming up with themes for posts and editing them, but because I was working at a startup, I only had time to work on my blog on the weekends. Even then, I'd often slack off because I was tired from the long nights of startup life. I remember receiving an email one day from someone who told me my site was down. It turns out that I had been hacked, which goes to show you how much care I was giving my side project.

One day after looking at analytics numbers for Femgineer, one of my employees at BizeeBee pointed out that I had a very engaged audience and gently nudged me to blog on a consistent basis. After looking at the numbers, I took my blog more seriously.

I made a *commitment* to blog once per month, and more often than that if I could. The more I blogged, the more people wanted me to blog, and other opportunities started popping up to the point where my side project had a mind of its own! Instead of trying to curtail it, I decided to give in and run an experiment at the end of 2012—5 years after I originally started the project!

People kept coming up to me and asking me things like: *"How do you build a product?" "How do you start a startup?" "How do you find teammates?"*

I decided to structure everything I'd learned into a course called "Lean Product Development"[7] and offer it online for 8 weeks. After the first iteration of the course I knew I was on to something, and decided it was time to transform my blog into a side business: an education company focused on helping people build tech products and companies.

While I was initially interested in starting a blog, much like how you are interested in building a product, I did things a bit ad hoc. I made incremental progress over a few years and this was enough, but when I decided to make a commitment to blogging consistently, things in my life actually started to transform.

Why?

Because I was more focused, and that translated to me caring about the quality of the work I produced. I thought about my audience, delegated by having people write guest posts, and set some simple goals I could stick to—like writing 1 post each month and eventually 1 per week.

Before I made an even bigger commitment to work on it full time, I set a goal to monetize the side business in 2013. Once I made sizable revenue (enough to support myself and an assistant) I decided that it was time to transform my side business into a real company.

This might seem like a reality only I've experienced, but I assure you, there have been a number of folks whom I've coached who have gone on to transform their ideas into side projects and businesses.

You might be wondering, *"How is this even possible?" "Can I realistically build a business by devoting a few hours a week?"*

In this chapter, I'm going to walk you through a number of strategies to help you set aside time to consistently work on your idea. If you can work through the exercises and make small weekly commitments, then you're sure to make progress through the rest of this guide.

And yes, you will be able to realistically create a product and eventually a business!

Section 1

Pet projects that interfere with your product

Too often, people dive right into building a product and then end up feeling overwhelmed by all the other things they have going on in their lives. The moment you feel overwhelmed, you start to lose motivation and your creative juices are gone.

Instead of assuming that we can just pile our plates high, let's take a step back and learn to recognize some of our pet projects to which we've already committed. I call them 'pets' because just like real pets, we've made a commitment to take care of these projects. And if we do a good job of taking care of them, they will nurture us in return.

Here are a few common pet projects:

- **Your day job**: I know it seems silly to call this a pet project, but just like walking a dog daily, you might have to keep your day job for a number of reasons. If it's a time-consuming day job, then it probably drains your energy by the end of the day, leaving you with little time to think about other things.

- **Family and personal commitments**: You may have other obligations, such as taking care of your family, and that's OK.

- **Other new and shiny projects**: You might be tempted to work on additional projects, thinking you can handle it all.

Let's dig into each of these and see what you may or may not be able to balance.

Pet Project 1: Your day job

It doesn't matter whether you love or hate your day job. What matters is whether you need it financially. Also, you might decide that you want the product you're developing to start as a side business. Either way, you'll need to come up with a plan to keep your day job and create the product on the side, or transition away from it over time. We'll go into greater detail on how to make this transition in the "Getting Working Capital" chapter. For now, let's just assume that you aren't going to quit your day job just yet or jump into building a product and company full time. And that's OK!

The reality is that products take time to build, and it takes companies a while to become profitable. So unless you've set aside a sizable amount of working capital and savings to cover your personal living expenses, you run the risk of running out of money before you can get your product into the hands of customers.

While many people seek investment to make full time product building easier, investors are becoming more demanding. They used to fund vaporware. Now it's only possible to receive funding for vaporware if you're a serial entrepreneur who has had a successful exit. For the rest, investors won't even bother talking to you unless you have a working prototype, customers, and often some sizable revenue.

Whether you choose to get funding or not, you'll need to validate your idea and know that it's OK to work on it while keeping your day job!

The only caveat is if you work for a company that prohibits any outside work, then unfortunately you can't do this simultaneously. If you're at all concerned, check with your employer. However, don't let this become a barrier to pursuing your idea! It may mean that you need to start saving up so that you can do your own thing full time.

This approach also works if you are reading this book with the goal of creating a product within your existing company. The only difference is that now you'll need to get buy-in from your company and figure out how the project aligns with its business goals. You'll need to do that whether or not you're launching within your existing company as you recruit technical talent and create your own product roadmap, which I'll cover in future chapters.

Whichever path you decide to follow, the next section will help you start to carve out both time and mental space to work on your product idea.

Pet Project 2: Family and personal commitments

If you already have more than 1 side project that takes up your free time—things like remodeling your house, coaching your kid's soccer league, or learning iPhone development—ask yourself whether now is the time to take on an additional project.

Why?

You're overloading your circuits!

To be creative and to think creatively, your mind needs a lot of rest and relaxation. That translates to about 8 hours of sleep and some relaxation time when you're awake. Overcommitting only causes anxiety that constricts the flow of blood to the brain and ultimately inhibits your creativity.

Even if you know this, you might still take on multiple projects to rev up your creative juices. You like to work under pressure!

The truth is, your prefrontal cortex is only capable of doing serious mental work for short bursts of time. If everything you do requires your prefrontal cortex, and you are constantly context-switching, then you'll tire it out and be ineffective!

You've probably already experienced this if you've ever felt scatterbrained when you sit down to work on an idea, because there are a number of other things we think we need to get done as well. *"Oh, I've gotta pick up the kids." "Need to get milk!" "Gotta take the dog for a walk." "Need to email my boss."*

These other thoughts prevent you from thinking clearly and creatively, and this is also one of the causes of feeling overwhelmed.

In addition, working under pressure constantly elevates the levels of adrenaline in your body. You get a surge of energy, but having these constant surges eventually depletes your adrenaline reserves. This leaves you feeling exhausted and eventually leads to burnout. The last thing you want is to burn out just when you're getting started!

The real way to rev up your creative juices is to make sure you are well rested and have a clear head before pursuing a new project. This gives your prefrontal cortex time to recuperate.

My sincere recommendation before digging into the exercises in this book is to finish the projects you've already started or delegate them to someone else who is interested. You'll be pleasantly surprised to find out that other people want to take over your projects or, at the very least, help!

Once you've completed some of the projects on your plate, come back and we'll focus on your product idea.

Pet Project 3: Other shiny projects

It's always tempting to take on additional projects because you know you can do it! However, you have to ask yourself: are you doing it because you're genuinely interested in this new project? Or are you:

- Afraid of missing out on the opportunity?

- Thinking that the other projects on your plate got too difficult or just plain boring?

If you are a person who is open, then opportunities are going to keep coming around, and that's a good thing! You can try to find alignment with your idea. But if alignment doesn't exist, then you have to politely decline these other projects for now in order to truly transform your idea into a product. The threat of shiny new projects is a real one and can distract you from your mission. If you feel like it's bound to happen, then you'll need to take the time to understand why you're choosing to move on to something new before completing the existing project. Ask yourself the following:

- Does it require expertise you don't have?

- Do you feel like it has lost some of the spark that it once used to have?

- Is it just no longer challenging?

- Do you want to be a starter and then hand off projects? There is nothing wrong with that—it just means you need to plan ahead!

All projects have at least 20% boring built in. You can either push through it or find someone to delegate it to. I know it seems like I keep saying "delegate," but there are people out there who want to help. They are eager to take on a new project and do some grunt work if they think it will be worthwhile. Like I mentioned before, you'll need to plan ahead if you want to offload projects.

Exercise 2.1: List your current 'pets.'

Objective: Take stock of all your current projects.

Directions: Remember, pet projects can include:

- Your day job

- Family and personal commitments

- Other shiny projects

Keep your list handy; we'll revisit it in the next exercise.

Let's move on to how you can dedicate time and mental space to pursue your product idea and complete the exercises in this guide. I'll be walking you through some additional exercises in this chapter to figure out how much time you can realistically set aside *consistently.*

Once you've done these exercises, you'll still need to take stock weekly, noting if this is indeed the amount of time you can commit to consistently or whether you need to change it up periodically.

I know it seems really dry and boring, but unfortunately we have to do this so that you know you can do the exercises in the following chapters and transform your idea into a product! I am a firm believer in both incremental progress and following through, because both lead to breakthroughs.

Section 2

Check your commitment level

Most people give up on their ideas way too early because they aren't focused and committed, but they place the blame on the idea not being "good." The reality is that they were *interested*, but not *committed*.

Commitment to a project doesn't mean investing 100 hours per week; it's not yet a full-time job. If it already is for you, that's awesome, and full speed ahead! Otherwise, I'm going to have you approach it as a side project.

It will require an investment of serious time. When I say "serious time," I mean time when you are focused on a particular task as it relates back to your idea. It could be 30 minutes a day, 1 hour a week, or half a day on the weekend. Often, short spurts are enough.

The time interval you want to commit to depends on how much time you have and when you know you focus best. If you're mentally exhausted, take a break; don't beat your brain against your idea! I can guarantee you'll make more progress once your mind has had time to relax.

The key to making progress on your idea is to set aside a consistent amount of time, and if for some reason you get derailed, you can get right back into it the following week! This is easier said than done, so at the end of this chapter, I am going to give you a step-by-step process, and I promise it will be simple.

We've covered the pet projects, so let's dig into other distractions and learn some strategies and tactics you can use to jump over them and follow through with your project.

Tactic 1: Create physical and mental space

Take the time to understand the ideal conditions where you do your best thinking. If you cannot think in a coffee shop, don't go to a coffee shop! If you cannot think at home because there are distractions, find another place. Create and find the space you need to work effectively.

I'm not telling you to remodel! Libraries can be great places to work, or you could book a conference room for an hour.

Also, take the time to let loved ones know you need this time. Their support will make all the difference, and it's important to let them know why you may be reducing the amount of time you can dedicate to them while you focus on your project.

Once again, this is easier said than done. I'm simply encouraging you to form a habit with your idea. If you can commit to even 1 hour a week, that's great. The key is to avoid coming up with excuses, such as: *"Oh, this Sunday I'm just too tired," "Oh, I'll start next week,"* and *"Who is going to know if I skip this time?"*

Everyone has days when they are tired or just feeling uninspired. The thing about inspiration is that you can reinvigorate it by doing just a little. So if you feel like you're having an off day, start a task and set a timer for 15 minutes. If at the end of the 15 minutes you're still not into it, then your brain just may very well be exhausted. But if after those 15 minutes you find flow, keep going!

Sometimes things come up and you may miss a day you've committed to working on your idea. That's OK. As I said before, get back on your regular schedule after a break. Return to the physical and mental space where your entire being is focused on your project.

Tactic 2: Carve out a consistent amount of time

To make it easier to focus your time on performing the steps I'm giving you, I want you to comb through your existing to-do list. Figure out the tasks that you could possibly delegate or automate, or even hire someone to do them if you think it's affordable.

If you wind up discovering 1-2 hours a week of time to spend on your idea, great. If it's 5-10, wonderful! More hours don't always lead to better results. It's better to have a few focused hours a week dedicated to making progress than waste half a day in a daze.

Second, I want you to come up with a weekly interval, because often times people have commitments to their day jobs that take a lot of time and focus. It might just not be possible to work on your idea every day, and that's OK.

As you get started with the exercises in this guide, you'll initially need to buckle down and see how it feels to set aside this time for a few weeks and then adjust accordingly. The goal is to arrive at an amount of time that is realistic and consistent.

Tactic 3: Take breaks

I want you to take breaks! If you just rush through this guide and read it like a book, then either you're super productive and seeing immediate results, or you're skipping key validation steps.

Take breaks to let your mind rest and give yourself time to complete the important exercises in this guide. Not every exercise can be performed in 15-30 minutes. Many of the exercises are experiments, which means that you'll have to wait for results to come in. I will provide suggestions for how long things should take. If you end up taking twice as long—or even 5 times as long—that's fine!

Now, let's get started with an exercise to help you assess your commitments, carve out time for your project, and follow through with it.

Exercise 2.2: Discover how much time you have to work on your product idea.

Objective: Estimate how long your current pet projects take, and discover time to work on your idea.

Directions:

1. Go back to the list of pet projects you created in Exercise 2.1. How much time do they take up, and what's their frequency?

   Here's an example of mine:

   - **Yoga** 3-5 times a week, 2 hours
   - **Running** 2 times a week, 45 minutes
   - **Work** 5 times a week, 8 hours
   - **Sleep** 7 times a week, 8 hours

- **Cooking dinner** 2 times a week, 30 minutes
- **Date night** once a week, 2-3 hours
- **Writing** 3-4 hours a week

2. **Highlight things you've committed to that will be ending soon, and how much time they are currently taking, so you can repurpose that time.**

- **Writing book** (July 31st) 3-4 hours a week

3. **Acknowledge time sinks.**

Certain activities waste far more time than is necessary. What are your personal time sinks?

Now, don't conflate entertainment with time sinks. If you spend an hour on Facebook and need that mental break, then take it!

But if you find that you're just wasting time checking your email constantly or lounging around doing whatever, ask yourself if you can repurpose some of that time.

If you're not sure whether you have time sinks, use an app like RescueTime[8] to track how long you take to perform a task.

4. **Cross off things that you may be interested in but feel like you can put on the back burner.**

For example, a year ago I put studying French on the back burner. While I wanted to learn, I just didn't have the mental bandwidth and had other priorities that I needed to focus on.

Please realize that putting things on the back burner doesn't mean that you cannot revisit them later!

Next, remember those shiny projects that belong to other people? Get comfortable saying NO to them. Once again, this is easier said than done. Try this out with a commitment you'd like to cross off your list or with a new responsibility that might come your way:

"Hey Person X, I think your Project Y is great, but I'm afraid I don't have time right now to do it justice, and honestly I'll just be holding you back. I've got a few things on my plate that I need to focus on and finish."

How does this feel to you? Do you feel guilty about saying no? Be OK with saying no politely, and do not let them or your mind guilt trip you into doing the project. You have to be firm with yourself and others if you want to stay focused!

5. How much time did you discover you have?

    Look at the items you crossed out and calculate how much extra time you found. The quantity doesn't really matter. Even if you discovered that you have 20-30 minutes per day or week, that's still great!

6. Can you commit to that time interval? What would the frequency of your commitment be? Daily, weekly, or monthly?

    If you find that you're tired when you're working on the idea, take some time to figure out when you think optimally. For me, it's the mornings between 6 a.m. to 9 a.m., and usually at the beginning of the week. By the end, my brain is fried!

7. **Stay accountable.**

Hold yourself accountable to achieving your goals. Here's how to do it: each week, take stock of whether or not you worked on your idea and how much time you spent on it. If you did, that's awesome! If not, why? Perhaps you got sick, and that is completely understandable; just get back on track the next week. Or, did a time sink or another commitment hold you back? Ultimately, you want to have a long running streak.

Pro tip: If you struggle with holding yourself accountable, then get someone else to do it. Pick someone who's strong-willed!

8. **Recruit teammates.**

Just because you're working on an idea on the side doesn't mean you have to go at it alone! I'd encourage you to recruit some partners, especially in areas where you might feel like you lack expertise.

Once you free up your mind and attention to focus on your goals, the sky is the limit. That's why it's so important to complete these exercises before moving on. Once you're ready, we'll learn how to build an audience and validate your idea.

Exercise 2.3: Schedule a weekly check-in with yourself.

Objective: Form a weekly habit of checking the progress you're making on your idea. The goals of this exercise are to keep a running log of your progress, identify any times you weren't able to make progress, and make note of the reasons. If you're getting stuck, make a note to help you get unstuck and stay motivated!

It might seem super simple and maybe even silly right now, but I assure you that by building up this habit, you will be more likely to focus and follow through.

Directions:

- If you are using Gmail for email then I want you to install the Boomerang plugin.[9]

- Once it's installed, open up an email, enter your email address in the to field, and set the subject line to: *tyi check-in* week # (replace # with the week number).

- Copy and paste the questions below:

    1. *How much time did you spend on your idea this week?*
    2. *If you didn't spend any time this week, why not?*
    3. *Will you be able to set aside the same amount of time next week? If not, why not?*
    4. *If you worked on your idea this week, what were the specific tasks you did and were there any results (doesn't matter if they were positive or negative)?*
    5. *Is there anything you are stuck on? What is it?*
    6. *If you did get stuck, who do you know that could help you, and what is the specific help you need from them? Or do you need to do some thinking or research on your own?*
    7. *Set 1-2 goals for the following week (e.g., "Do Exercise 1 in chapter 3.")*

- Instead of hitting the send button, hit the send later button, and set it to 1 week.

- When you get the email a week later, answer the questions in 15 minutes or less, and schedule an email with the same list of questions for the next week.

If you don't have Gmail or Boomerang, then pick your favorite calendaring or to-do app and set a weekly reminder.

I've had every single person I mentor do this exercise. The results have been that they've shipped products on time, raised successful crowdfunding campaigns, and gotten themselves out of periodic but natural slumps.

 Review

I want you to approach your idea as a side project and use the exercises in this book to transform it into a product. However, before we can begin you'll need to take care of pet projects, account for any distractions that might hold you back, and make a realistic assessment of how much time you have each week. Finally, you'll want to do a weekly check-in with yourself to take stock of what you've accomplished and identify anything you're stuck on.

Know that you are in control of the pace and that consistency and incremental progress leads to big wins!

Interview with Brittany Forsyth, Head of Human Relations at Shopify.

Shopify[10] is a commerce platform that allows anyone to sell products online, in-store, and everywhere in between.

Shopify offers a professional online storefront, a payment solution to accept credit cards, a point-of-sale application to power retail sales, and a card reader to process credit card transactions through a mobile phone. Shopify currently powers over 100,000 retailers in 150 different countries, including Tesla Motors, Gatorade, Forbes, Amnesty International, Encyclopædia Britannica, CrossFit, and many more.

Shopify was founded in 2006 and has received $122 million in Series A and B funding from Bessemer Venture Partners, FirstMark Capital, Felicis Ventures, and Georgian Partners.[11]

I chose to interview Brittany because I wanted you to see the perspective of an early employee of a startup and learn how you can add value to someone else's idea. As you read through the interview, you'll learn why Brittany chose to join Shopify when it was a 20-person startup. You'll also learn how Shopify's culture has evolved over the years.

Poornima: "Hi Brittany! Thanks for taking the time to do this interview with me. Let's begin by talking about Shopify's early days, and then talk about how you got involved."

Brittany: "Sure. Back in 2004, Tobias Lütke had just moved from Germany to live in Ottawa, Canada. He loved to snowboard and wanted to start selling snowboards online. Frustrated with the e-commerce options available at that time, and being a programmer at heart, he decided to build the software himself. He then quickly realized the value wasn't in selling snowboards but the actual software, and Shopify officially launched in 2006."

Poornima: "That's a pretty cool epiphany, how did he get there?"

Brittany: "At the time, there were only a few options for selling online. You either had to spend hundreds of thousands of dollars to build your own site or use a very generic and boring template. Neither were very customizable. So he knew there was room in the market."

Poornima: "Got it. So, let's talk about how you got involved with Shopify."

Brittany: "I went to school for human resources and I was looking for a position. My dad, who was pretty active on Twitter, showed me a tweet by Tobias. Tobias was looking for an office manager and my dad encouraged me to reach out. I had no idea what to expect. It wasn't in my field, so I took a chance and went for it anyway. I arrived for an interview and immediately fell in love with the company. I knew they were going to grow. I pitched them on starting off as an office manager, and eventually doing HR work."

Poornima: "What happened next?"

Brittany: "I was an office manager for two months but then I switched to recruiting, onboarding new employees, and figuring out compensation structures. It was a really creative period."

Poornima: "How did the company grow over time?"

Brittany: "We were doubling in size each year and now we're at about 500 employees in three offices: Ottawa, Toronto, and Montreal. We have about 115,000 merchants all over the world. The majority are in North America."

Poornima: "And how was Shopify funded?"

Brittany: "Initially we were bootstrapped, with a little bit of help from friends and family. Since 2010, we have received funding from some notable VCs. We raised $7 million in a Series A in 2010, $15 million in a Series B in 2011 and $100 million in a Series C in 2013.

Poornima: "Who was your initial customer and how did that change over time?"

Brittany: "Initially our customers were entrepreneurs and small- to medium-sized businesses that were looking for a way to sell online. Today, even though the majority of our merchants would still identify themselves in that group, many of our customers have grown alongside Shopify and now sell millions of dollars worth of products a year. Also, in 2013, we decided to move from being an e-commerce company to a commerce company. We expanded our product offering and entered into physical retail with our point-of-sale solution. From this, we have acquired many brick-and-mortar stores who use Shopify just for their physical locations.

Poornima: "Yeah, I know that e-commerce startups that are evaluating building versus buying software should consider using Shopify, but it's cool to know that other businesses could also benefit. Let's switch gears and talk about your culture today. Is Shopify primarily based in Ottawa?"

Brittany: "We have about 70 employees in Toronto, 25 in Montreal, and 400+ in Ottawa. We're hiring all over Canada, and we've also started hiring remotely. Things have pretty much stayed the same, because we have the original leaders from when the company began. They have set the tone. We built a culture of autonomy; people can do what they want, and they are always willing to learn. That's still ingrained in our value system but we have refined a few things as we've grown."

Poornima: "Can you give me an example?"

Brittany: "We used to say: *Ship Fast.* Now we say: *Ship sustainably fast.* At a certain point we realized we needed to think about scaling and optimizing for the future, while innovating."

Poornima: "That's great, and yes, as your team grows, you do have to be concerned about building at a sustainable pace."

Brittany: "Yes, we reassess all the time because things change every month."

Poornima: "You've also been doing quite a bit of outreach, right?"

Brittany: "Yes, we do hackathons in the office, and employees can hold meetups. We provide the backing they need, and in return we just ask that employees are the ones who support it and keep it going."

Poornima: "Any final takeaways for our readers who are interested in being an early-stage startup employee and working on someone else's idea before they go off and pursue their own?"

Brittany: "Yes. There has to be a fit. Part of that is having an overwhelming desire to think and work on the idea. It's OK to be a little scared, but you have to learn to embrace the chaos and risk. You don't need to know everything. My naivety made me thrive. I was right out of school, I didn't have a foundation, and that made me take a fresh look and ask myself, 'How would I do this?' Never underestimate what you can bring to the table. Finally, state your opinion without fear and be ready and open to feedback."

Poornima: "Those are great takeaways, Brittany. Thank you, and I wish both you and Shopify continued success!"

Just to recap, here's what we learned from Brittany Forsyth:

- **You can join an early-stage startup and make an impact on someone else's idea.** Brittany joined Shopify when they were just 20 employees. She has helped shape the company culture and recruited talented employees.

- **You don't need to know everything.** A beginner's mindset can bring a fresh perspective and approach. Never underestimate what you can bring to the table.

- **You can be scared, but you've got to learn to embrace the constant change.** As the change occurs, you will need to reassess values and processes.

Chapter 3

Mitigating Market Risk

Back in June, I was at a conference called PreMoney,[12] which was hosted by 500 Startups.[13] One of the angel investors, Jeff Clavier, who was also an investor in Mint.com, told us about his famous **"three asses rule"**: a smart-ass team building a kick-ass product in a big-ass market. Clavier uses this rule to determine whether or not he will invest in a company.

However, Clavier also admitted that this rule has caused him to overlook investments in companies like AirBnB and Kickstarter. The reason he overlooked them was because they initially didn't fit these three criteria. The market demand was pretty nascent.

Over time, these companies have been able to successfully grow their respective markets, but it took a combination of educating customers and building a kick-ass product.

When you're building for a young and growing market, you are actually taking a rather large risk. The market may develop over time or demand might fizzle out. Moreover, you are starting with a small base of customers, and instead of waiting for people to adopt your product, you have to grow the market by educating potential customers about your product's value proposition and benefits.

However, this won't happen immediately, because it requires customers to change their behavior. If you've ever tried to break an old habit or try something new, you've probably experienced a period of discomfort, which might have caused you to either quit immediately, or, at the very least, question your effort. This is exactly how customers, who have yet to adopt your product, feel. They aren't sure, they worry about the product's benefits, and the transition process causes them to question the worth of your product.

This can wreak havoc on your product's growth trajectory, and it's up to you to decide whether you want to take a risk. The risk could potentially have a major upside: your product could be the market leader and grow the market. Or, it could have the potential downside of demand fizzling out over time.

How do you choose what to do?

Case Study

Pursuing an uncertain path with BizeeBee

At the end of 2012, I was in a really tight spot. My startup, BizeeBee, had run out of capital, but we were making money. It was just not enough to cover everyone's salaries. I had to make a tough call: shut it down, get acqui-hired, or keep it running. I decided to keep it running, because I kept seeing the signs of more and more customers who were sticking around for months and years!

In the midst of a lot of uncertainty, I decided to take a pretty big risk. Instead of selling the company, I'd keep it running mostly on my own. Almost 2 years later, I'm happy to report that I made the right choice!

The big risk I took was mitigated by 3 priorities that I had set from day one of building BizeeBee:

- A simple product that customers could onboard themselves.

- Test-driven development to ensure as close to bug-free code as possible so that we wouldn't have too many customer complaints or churn.

- Going after a very specific market segment: independent yoga and fitness studios.

Section 1

There is uncertainty in any size market

Whether you're pursuing this idea on your own or within a larger organization, there is a level of uncertainty involved because you're pursuing something new and are unsure how it will play out. Uncertainty often makes us feel like we're taking on a really big risk, and it can be unsettling.

This is often one of the stages where people quit, because they think the risk factors are too hard to overcome, such as growing a nascent market.

In larger markets, where there may be one big competitor or many competitors, people worry and wonder, *"What is the point of building something if it's already been done?"*

However, I want to help you work through this type of thinking by understanding how to mitigate personal risk when introducing a product into a market, whether it's one that is young or developed.

If you have a business or marketing background, you might already be familiar with some of these concepts, so please bear with me. I'm hoping you'll learn something new! And if you're technical, then you'll need to pay close attention to these lessons, because the techniques covered are instrumental in attracting customers to your product and ultimately finding product-market fit.

Developing market awareness

Market awareness is not just about understanding what is happening today. It's also about being aware of what has happened in the past, and while we cannot predict the future based on the past, we should at least have enough knowledge to see and understand trends.

 Case Study

Battling 800lb gorillas for market share at Mint.com

When we were getting started with Mint.com, we knew we had two formidable competitors: Intuit and Microsoft.

Intuit's product Quicken and Microsoft's product Money were both shrink-wrapped software that helped people manage their personal finances.

In 2005, we saw signs that the market was moving away from shrink-wrapped software and towards SaaS (software as a service) web-based products. We were able to spot these trends by witnessing the ever-increasing adoption of Facebook and Google.

In the late '90s, people were really wary of buying things and doing business online, but by 2005, we noticed that people were getting over their reservations about using online products. The greatest tell-tale sign was the popularity of online banking.

However, our competitors hadn't yet developed SaaS products; they were still building as if it were the '90s. This might have been guided by their customers' reluctance to change. It could also have been the momentum they had developed internally, constraining them to continue to build a product a certain way rather than explore new methods, such as building and distributing software online.

We also knew that Quicken had end-of-life'd their Mac product, annoying a large portion of their customer base.

Neither competitor had a SaaS product, nor were they building one. That, coupled with signs of growth and demand for SaaS products, presented us with a prime opportunity!

With all this information, we knew that we could release our product online, making it compatible across multiple platforms.

The opportunity available to us outweighed the risk factors, and having knowledge of the market gave us a clear-cut strategy.

Had we let our fear of taking a risk consume us, we wouldn't have been as successful as we had been. But following the market and positioning ourselves relative to our competitors mitigated a lot of risk.

If you can't beat 'em, join 'em!

Eventually, Microsoft end-of-life'd its product, Microsoft Money, while Quicken tried to compete with us by releasing Quicken Online. It was not well received. Its growth numbers stagnated for months.

Eventually, Intuit grew jealous of Mint.com's growth. In 2008 they called us out on it. Our response was, *"Thanks for noticing!"* Then, in 2009, they made two acquisition offers. Mint.com's founder, Aaron Patzer, accepted the second offer, and the rest was history!

A disclaimer: We were pretty fortunate in having a clear vision and executing on it, but there are times when companies don't always have a clear-cut strategy or have to change course based on what is going on in the market. This causes people to pivot (i.e., change direction to find a course that will work). I'll be covering pivoting in a future chapter on product iteration.

Section 3

Developing domain expertise

If your product idea is based on you scratching your own itch, that's great! But in order to validate that there is demand for it in the market, you need to take the time to understand other people's experiences and design a general solution. I'll explain how to do this in Chapter 5.

One of the key ingredients to building a successful product in a market that is either large or nascent is having a level of domain expertise. This isn't to say you cannot build a product for a market you don't know about. I'm only suggesting that if you don't have domain expertise, then you take the time to do some research.

Too often, people skip this step and jump right into building a product for a customer base thinking that they just know what the users want. This approach is sure to backfire! And you'll experience it too if you put the product in front of customers: they either won't want it or get how to use it.

I'm not saying you need to be an expert in a particular industry, but you do need to understand the nuances of how customers feel in that particular market. Those nuances are what your competitors or potential competitors might not be aware of. In the case of Mint.com, we understood the growing demand in SaaS products and people's desire for a very simple tool that helps them manage their money.

Section 4

The power of positioning

It doesn't matter whether you are building a product for a nascent market or a crowded one. What matters most is how you position the product relative to others. Positioning is the process of creating an image or identity in the customer's mind. Having a level of market awareness helps you develop a position in the market.

You can position based on any of the following factors: price, packaging, promotion, distribution, and competition.

Your product's position in the market signals to customers how it is different from alternatives. This, in turn, helps to identify and attract customers.

People often jump into building and skip positioning altogether, thinking it's just a waste of time or that their product applies to everyone.

They fear that going after a targeted segment will alienate people.

Well, they're half right.

Case Study

How customer interviews led to insights for BizeeBee

When I was getting started with BizeeBee, I had been a yoga practitioner for 6 years and had volunteered at studios. However, I didn't know what it was like to own or run a studio. So, I spent time interviewing a number of owners, instructors, and business managers across the country. I uncovered some similar sentiments that people had toward technology: everything seemed complicated, required training, and needed a large investment of time—something that business owners lack.

Taking the time to conduct these interviews led me to develop a deeper understanding of their needs. What they needed was something simple.

Eventually, that became our tagline: *"BizeeBee simplifies your studio."* We later changed it to *"Membership management made easy,"* but it's still the same theme.

I'll go into detail on how you can conduct customer interviews and gain valuable insights in Chapter 5.

While their product and vision might apply to everyone eventually, appealing to everyone from the beginning is problematic because

- **People have nuanced needs.** Even if you think that your product applies to everyone, people might have some nuanced needs that you may not be able to address initially. When you are getting started, you are constrained by how much you can build and the value you can add. You may need to build out more of a solution that appeals to everyone. This doesn't mean you need to build everything at once. Instead, you need to focus on attracting those who have needs you can meet. You can build a loyal following by addressing nuanced needs. Word will get out! And, once you see clear signs of demand growing, you can build more to attract another group of customers.

- **People are risk averse.** If you are introducing a new product in the market or are a new company, customers may question your product's benefits and your company's credibility. The last thing they want is to buy a product that will be recalled or is supported by a company that will go under! Once again, having a concentrated message that appeals to a subset of customers, clearly highlights your product's benefits, and conveys the company's credibility will lead to adoption.

- **People struggle with change of behavior.** Some might not be willing to adopt your product because it requires them to change their lifestyles. They want to take the time to understand how your product appeals to their existing habits and behavior. They want to see how others will use it first. You'll need to continue to educate them on your product's benefits using case studies from other customers to compel them.

Section 5

Vertical market adoption

If you look at products that have had the widest adoption over time, you'll notice that they all began by targeting a niche. One classic example is Facebook. It started out as a social network for students at top-tier colleges in the US. As interest grew, Facebook expanded to other colleges, but kept its focus on the college market. This vertical market strategy led them to develop a loyal base.

Two years after their launch, they opened up their platform to serve the general public.

This strategy can be particularly beneficial in a market that is crowded with competitors or has one large incumbent. For example, as new social networks come out in the market, you'll notice that they focus on niches to avoid competing with Facebook directly. Take, for example, SnapChat, which is focused on teens and tweens. It doesn't exclude other people from using it. They just targeted an initial group they thought the product would resonate with.

It's easy to get tripped up and differentiate just based on features and functionality of a product. But taking the time to develop a position that targets a niche will help you attract an initial set of customers known as **early adopters**, who can serve you well in getting the word out about the product. The beauty of attracting the right set of customers is that once you've met their needs, they will go on to evangelize your product. They eventually become known as "earlyvangelists"[14] because they evangelize your product to others. Word-of-mouth marketing is the most powerful means of product adoption. Potential customers are more likely to trust their close friends and acquaintances than your marketing message. Hence earlyvangelists will be key to your success.

If you've already built a product and are left wondering why no one seems interested, it's very likely that it's not actually a product problem but a positioning one. You haven't clearly conveyed whom the product is for and what the benefits are. You might also have picked the wrong channels to advertise—more on that in Chapter 4 and Chapter 10.

A good test is to determine whether you're talking too much about the features and functionality of your product, rather than whom it's for and how your product benefits a customer. You'll know if potential customers are asking you if it has XYZ feature.

If you're interested in learning even more about positioning, I'd highly recommend reading Al Ries and Jack Trout's book, *Positioning*.[15] I read it over 5 years ago, and it has left a very lasting impression on me.

Let's switch gears and talk about how we develop a position. There are 4 steps involved:

1. Competitive Analysis

2. Market Sizing

3. Identifying Neglected and Growing User Segments

4. Differentiation

Section 6

Competitive analysis

Start by defining the industry you are in. You might actually be in two industries, because that is the nature of technology. Perhaps you disrupt an industry and are also a part of the high-tech industry. For example, Mint.com was in the software industry (part of high tech) and it was also in the financial services industry.

Next, identify competitors within the industry, both large and small. At Mint, our competitors were Intuit, Microsoft, and some smaller startups like Wesabe and Geezeo.

The third step when doing competitive analysis is to get a bird's eye view of the various types of customers and the benefits they are seeking. When it comes to personal finances, some people care about one or all of the following: saving money, making money, and spending it wisely. Hence, they are looking for benefits as it relates to these three larger goals. *What are they*

Next, you'll need to understand the key success factors in the industry. This requires getting a historical perspective of how competitors formed the industry.

When we studied our competitors, we learned that the founder of Intuit, Scott Cook, had initially approached people who were PC users back in the '80s. These early adopters of technology were affluent but still cared about managing their finances.

Cook went door-to-door to conduct usability tests. This approach took a while for him to scale the business to the multi-billion dollar company that it is today.

Fast forward to 2005. The presence of the Internet made distribution and evangelizing the product at Mint a lot easier than it was for Cook back in the '80s!

Some other things to think about when positioning a product are adoption and the rate of innovation.

If you are operating in a market where people are used to the status quo in terms of products and technology, then introducing a new product will be difficult. This has certainly been the case for me with BizeeBee. It's been a slower growth trajectory because a lot of studio owners have become accustomed to managing their businesses on Excel or paper and pen.

It's not until they see the need for software to improve their operational efficiencies that they are willing to change their management practices. And often times, that is spurred on by competition they feel from other studios.

Another trend to keep track of is your competitors' rate of innovation. If they are slow to innovate, you can capitalize on that. At Mint we certainly benefited from the fact that Intuit was still building shrink-wrapped software, and we focused our efforts on building a web-based solution.

You've probably seen the same. Many companies today often skip building a web app and go straight to mobile, capitalizing on consumers' ever-increasing rate of smartphone adoption.

Finally, there is a need to think about distribution as it relates to customer reach. *What types of consumers are emerging whom your competitors don't know about or have failed to serve?*

In the yoga market, the growth of independent studio owners and private instructors who are building studio-less yoga businesses has outpaced those opening big-box studios. I spotted this trend early on and decided to keep the focus on those entering the market or operating smaller studios. Most of BizeeBee's competitors offer bigger end-to-end products that are overkill for small studios and yoga businesses.

Exercise 3.1: Perform competitive analysis on your competitors.

Objective: Get a sense of how customers feel about existing competitors.

Directions: Take 3 competitors, dig into what people love and hate about their products, and list the key characteristics of these people.

You can do this research by using something like Twitter's search box to see how people feel about a product. Here are some tweets I found from Quicken users when I did a search.

Michael Phipps @mphipps72 · May 7
@Quicken I upgrade to 2014 and now my online updates dont work. Thanks for taking my money and wasting my time troubleshooting your product

Figure 3.1

Randy Brock @RandyBrock · Mar 22
I feel like I was completely bamboozled by Intuit. Forced to upgrade to **Quicken** 2014 to keep **online** services, which don't work on upgrade.

Figure 3.2

The key isn't to just go off of the negative sentiment. You'll want to follow up and find out what they also love about the product. This is important, because even if someone hates a product, they might be loyal to it out of comfort. It's up to you to figure out if you can displace the competitor's solution or work in tandem. To do this, you'll need to understand how willing people are to switch.

By doing this, you'll understand who the people are that your competitors are servicing. The next phase is to understand who your competitor has neglected to service completely.

Market sizing

Another mistake that people make is going down a path of an idea, only to realize that there is a very small market for it. As I've mentioned, it's OK to be in a small market, as long as demand is growing and you've seen the trend over time.

If your goal is to build a company and possibly attract investors, then you need to take the time to do a market sizing exercise. Most investors, like Clavier and especially venture capitalists, are only willing to invest if they know you are tackling a problem within a large market. There are some who are willing to take a risk if you can show that the market is growing quickly. I'll get into the reasons behind this Chapter 14.

There are 3 components of market sizing:

1. **Total addressable market (TAM):** *How big is the market you are currently in? How quickly is it growing?*

2. **Served addressable market (SAM):** *Within the bigger market, whom do you actually service? How quickly is that segment growing?*

3. **Target Market:** *Whom will you service first? Who will most likely be early adopters?*

OK, I know this is a lot to digest, but stay with me; these are necessary steps if we're going to get to our goal of attracting customers!

Exercise 3.2: Discover the size of your target market.

Objective: Identify a potential target market and its size.

Directions: Now it's your turn to answer the following questions:

1. **Total addressable market (TAM):** *How big is the market you are currently in? How quickly is it growing?*

2. **Served addressable market (SAM):** *Within the bigger market, whom do you actually service? How quickly is that segment growing?*

3. **Target Market:** *Whom will you service first? Who will most likely be early adopters?*

The overall goal of doing market sizing is to be aware of market trends, and discover new customer segments that might have looked into your competitor's solution only to discover that it doesn't meet their needs, and hence become a neglected segment.

Exercise 3.3: Identify neglected and growing customer segments.

Objective: To understand why current products aren't meeting the needs of customers and determine whether they are a neglected and/or growing customer segment.

Directions: If you've completed the competitive analysis exercise, the next step is to take a step back and make sure that you can answer these two questions:

1. **Why are there so many products?** Is the market growing, and in return, the demand for products within it? Or is it that most products are solving just a sliver of the problem, leaving customers unsatisfied and constantly searching for more?

2. **Why aren't there more products?** It could be that this is a new market or a very niche market. That is certainly the case for BizeeBee. It's operating in a niche market, but that doesn't mean that we cannot expand beyond yoga into other fitness verticals. Or, it could be that there is one major player who has outpaced others. Take, for example, Google with search and Facebook with social networking.

It's important to keep these factors in mind as you position your product.

 Case Study

BizeeBee's market size

I'll illustrate each of these using BizeeBee.

The total yoga market is a $22B market in the US, composed of products (yoga mats, apparel, etc.) and services like classes. This is the **total addressable market (TAM)**. BizeeBee is just focused on servicing yoga studios and yoga businesses. So the **served addressable market (SAM)** is 30K+ studios in the US. Within that, our target market is independent studios, which are 90%+ of the SAM.

As I've mentioned before, in the case of the former, you'll need to spend time educating people on the benefits of your solution and growing the market through those efforts.

In the case of the latter, you'll need to do more work unearthing your competitor's limitations and neglected customer segments, and innating past the products that have strong positions in the minds of customers.

Exercise 3.4: Focus on the needs of the neglected segment.

Objective: To identify if the neglected segment could potentially be early adopters.

Directions: Ask yourself the following questions:

1. Who doesn't the competitor "get?"

2. What will make this group loyal?

3. What will it take to convince them to try out your product: price, features, credibility, comfort?

It's often the neglected segment that is filled with early adopters for your product, but not always!

You'll still need to conduct customer interviews to make sure, and I'll cover how to do that in Chapter 5!

Section 8

Differentiation techniques

If you've done your market sizing, competitive analysis, and identified neglected and growing customer segments, then you're one step closer to differentiating your product and creating a solid position in the market for it.

However, whenever I talk about differentiation techniques, people are quick to ask me if they should be appealing to people's heads or their hearts. The truth is that customers make decisions based on a number of factors. Even those who are pretty emotional will often take the time to think through a decision, and those who usually think things through might decide to just follow their gut once in a while.

Hence when you're thinking about differentiating your product, you've gotta come back to the elements of positioning:

- Price

- Distribution

- Promotion

- Packaging a.k.a Design

- Competition

One final technique when it comes to differentiating your product is to decide whether you want to build a point tool or an integrated solution. Often this isn't a choice. When you are getting started you have to build something small, which could be a point tool that can be used alongside other products.

You can eventually transform your point tool into an integrated solution. In Chapter 13, I'll explain how this might actually be a type of pivot you'll want to consider.

This is how application hosting company Heroku[16] transformed itself.

It began by hosting web applications, and then to differentiate itself from other hosting companies like RackSpace[17] and EngineYard[18], it became a platform company. Instead of building everything to support web applications, their platform made it seamless for companies that were building infrastructure application products to offer their product. People who hosted their applications could choose these infrastructure products by just sliding a slider, and within seconds their applications would have the add-on. People chose add-ons such as logging, application performance monitoring, database support, etc.

In this particular case, Heroku changed its position over time, which will most likely happen to your product as well.

 ## Case Study

Mint.com's positioning strategy: product design + people

Back in 2005, when Aaron Patzer, the founder of Mint.com, was getting started on his idea, I was helping him brainstorm. I came up with the name while we were stuck in a snowstorm on our way to Tahoe.

Later I remember talking to my dad about the idea, and he said something like, *"Why are you interested in this? Quicken already exists!"*

While he did have a point, he didn't understand that there was room in the market for another product. People wanted something *simple.* Especially people who were tech savvy. They didn't want to spend hours getting themselves set up on a tool like Quicken, especially those who were young and wanted to spend more of their time enjoying life, not managing their finances!

That was proof enough for me. But, we weren't the only ones who knew this. One of our startup competitors, Wesabe, launched a year before us!

I was really nervous as I logged into their product. But after logging in, I realized that they weren't building what we were building. Their product was more around providing social advice around money management, and they required you to upload files from your bank. Our value proposition, however, was to make it so that you could login and automatically see all your financial data in one place, so you wouldn't have to do too much work. Mint would do all the heavy lifting for you!

This is the value proposition we put out into the world.

We didn't talk about what features we had, because honestly we didn't have a lot when we launched. It was pretty simple tool; you could see your bank and credit card accounts, and that was it. We eventually added to it, but the initial value proposition was clear and different enough to get people interested.

To differentiate ourselves, we thought about how we could add value, not just one additional feature.

(handwritten notes at top of page)
- create strong position
- Be aware of market
- Target - niche

Review

I started out by describing a level of risk that comes with pursuing an idea. However, you can mitigate that risk by having a level of market awareness and domain expertise. While those are necessary conditions, you still need to go through the exercise of creating a strong position for your product. In order to do that effectively you'll want to take the time to do some market sizing, conduct a competitive analysis, identify neglected or growing customer segments, and use all that you've learned to differentiate your product and company.

What you've validated in this chapter

If you completed the exercises in this chapter, then you should have validated the following:

- A market for your idea exists.

- There are neglected customer segments that your competitor is not satisfying or servicing.

Chapter 4

Building an Audience Before You Build Your Product

Once a year, I head over to New York City and spend a week there, usually around springtime because I am not a cold weather person; I was born in the tropics, raised in the Texas heat, and love to practice Bikram (hot) yoga 3-5 times a week!

My week is usually filled with business and fun. I get to hang out with my close friends, ride the subway around town to meet with BizeeBee customers, dine at delicious restaurants (I love the French food at Buvette[19] and the pizza at Otto[20]), and host a Femgineer Forum.

As my trip comes to an end, I always wish that my NYC friends lived in San Francisco or Palo Alto. But then I realize that they're different; they need the hustle and bustle of Manhattan, the seasons, and all the culture that the city has to offer. While I love the city, it's not for me. I need the 300+ days of sunshine in Palo Alto, California, to keep me happy and productive. I've grown to accept our differences and enjoy my time in NYC.

Figure 4.1 Walking through Central Park on a Sunday afternoon in May.

My friends and I are not the same; we have common shared values, but we enjoy living in different locations. The same is true of customers.

If your idea is based on a problem that you've experienced, you might quickly conclude that your customers are going to be exactly like you. You might just jump into building a product thinking you know exactly what the customer's needs are because of your own. That is a pretty big assumption to make.

The truth is that even if your customers have the same problem as you do, there are subtle nuances that you need to be aware of when building and designing a product. Those subtle nuances can dramatically affect how customers perceive, adopt, and use your product.

Joshua Brewer, the author of the popular blog 52 Weeks of UX, wrote a great post called "You Are NOT Your User."[21]

If your intention is to resell your product to others, then you have to take the time to validate the similarities and understand the differences between you and your customer.

Once again, you might feel like building something before talking to potential customers, thinking that they will be unwilling to talk to you unless you have something to show them. So, let me ask you two simple questions:

1. Do you read every book and then pay for it?

2. Do you wait for Amazon to ship you an item, then say, "Oh yes, this is exactly what I wanted," and only then pay for it?

I'm going to take a wild guess here and assume the answers are probably no. You pre-order a product, sometimes even before trying it out.

Well, that's exactly what your goal should be with your product: to get people to pre-order or pre-pay for it before they try it out!

Doing this verifies that there is actual demand. Otherwise, you're just speculating that there is a need, but customers may or may not be interested.

In the upcoming sections, I'll provide you with some initial steps to achieve this goal.

Section 1

File your product idea away and focus on having conversations with potential customers

It's often tempting to spend your time building a prototype. Perhaps you want to have something to show people so they'll take you more seriously. However, you'll be amazed at how receptive people are when it comes to hearing ideas.

Think about it this way: when was the last time a friend told you about some cool new product or service? Did they show it to you or did they just tell you what it was?

Most likely you were hanging out, and they told you what it was. You might still have felt like you needed to see it to believe it, but you probably got the gist of the idea. If they raved about it, then it possibly even piqued your curiosity enough to go and check it out later.

I know even after I mention this, you may be skeptical. So let me put it another way ... If you walk up to someone, whom you either know or don't know, with a tablet or laptop and show them what you've built, what do you think they'll say? Probably something like this:

"Oh I HATE green!"
"Is this just for Macs?"
"Is there a mobile app for it?"
"How much does it cost?"

This early in the game, these questions are not helpful. You do not want people to get obsessed with design, form factors, pricing, or any minutiae related to the product.

Honestly, the specifics of your idea don't matter right now.

What you really want is to take the time to have high-level conversations that give you an understanding of potential customers, such as who they are, what their needs are, and how they go about meeting their needs.

You want to know what's important to them because you can use that to refine your idea!

OK, I know what you're thinking: *"C'mon, Poornima, don't we need to talk about my idea? How is talking about their needs going to validate my idea?"*

Here's the thing. If you start talking about YOUR idea, then two things will happen:

1. **Confirmation bias.** You may confirm that someone has a problem based on your idea, but you won't confirm whether it's their highest-priority issue or understand what else is on their mind. You need to build up more context and a deep understanding of people who *might* be experiencing a problem that your idea is solving.

Taking the time to develop a deep understanding of individuals lets you get a sense of what is really important to them, which lets you refine your idea and its direction.

Later in this guide, we'll be talking about how to pare down features to put into a prototype. In order to pare down effectively, you need to get a head start understanding the priorities of your customers.

2. **People clam up when they're being sold to.** Have you ever received a call from a telemarketer trying to sell you something? What is the first thing you do? Click.

If you don't want someone to tune out during your initial meeting and you really want to have an honest dialogue, then keep the tablet, laptop, and your product idea to yourself! The goal at this stage is to understand who your audience is. To do that, you've gotta focus on getting to know the person you're talking to.

If you're concerned that they won't take a meeting because they don't know what you're up to, then give them a high-level description. Here's what we used to tell interview candidates when I was at Mint.com.

"Hi there! We are looking to build a simple solution that benefits budget-minded individuals. Would you be open to talking to us and sharing how you currently manage your finances?"

Notice I've kept it open-ended but provided enough context to get their interest.

Once they agree, I've got to follow up and schedule some time to chat, preferably in person.

If you still don't believe me, then maybe the story of one of my students from my Lean Product Development Course will drive the point home.[22]

Case Study

Hermione's hunch

Hermione is a product manager who has focused much of her career on creating products in the life sciences.

Based on her experiences, she had a hypothesis that private doctors were struggling to get patients to return to their clinics, and this was what was limiting their bottom lines.

She wanted to build a CRM (customer relationship management) solution that would track patient visits and then remind them that they needed to visit again. She was pretty hell-bent on building this even before talking to a single doctor because she thought they'd be more willing to talk to her if she came with a solution in hand. I encouraged her to go out, visit some private doctors, ask them what issues they are facing, and have them prioritize the issues.

Hermione was reluctant, but she humored me. She set off into Chicago, met with 3 private doctors, conducted interviews, and asked them about how they ran their businesses, the products they were currently using, and issues they faced daily.

When she got to the question of *"Do you struggle with getting patients to come back?"* they all said no and instead responded that they struggle with getting patients who do come back to pay their bills on time! The billing software they used wasn't solving this problem, and they were really in need of a better solution that would encourage patients to pay their bills punctually.

This was an eye-opening experience for Hermione, and she realized that she needed to shift her focus. Because she hadn't built anything yet, she felt like she hadn't wasted time or resources and could easily switch her focus.

You might be like Hermione and have a hunch about what your potential customers' needs are, but until you conduct that first interview, you cannot be sure.

In a future chapter, I'll dig into how to conduct this interview. For now, let's focus on some tactics for how you can start to build an audience.

Building an audience early on is going to make the product phases fly because you'll have a pool of customers you can recruit to provide you feedback.

Section 2

Tap into your existing network

In the last chapter, I talked about how it's prudent to have domain expertise and a strong network of people you can interact with when pursuing an idea. If you don't have either, then you need to go out, develop expertise, and build a network!

When I was starting BizeeBee, I didn't know how to run a yoga studio, but I had volunteered at one for 6 months. I also had many friends who were owners and instructors.

As I was developing the product idea for BizeeBee, I needed people to interview. So initially I recruited people I already knew: all my friends who were owners and instructors!

You might think that people who are your friends will give you only positive feedback. Yes, that's true. However, I made people take it seriously by telling them that my goal was to eventually build a product for them, one that they would pay for. Since they weren't going to get a free lunch, they were willing to give me frank feedback.

Some told me that they wouldn't use the product because it didn't suit the size of their business, but I did have a few who were willing to sign up, pay, and use it!

I also didn't take a "no" as a sign that I was at a dead end. Since I had taken the time to educate them on what I was doing, and because they knew that I was a credible person, I asked for referrals. I'd ask them if they knew 1-3 people whom they could introduce me to via email. Once I received the introduction, I followed up immediately.

take time to educate customer

This is how I went about building my initial audience base that eventually led to paying customers.

I also made it a point to start local, meeting people face-to-face as much as I could. While this may seem really labor intensive, it's necessary to have this level of a personal touch when you're getting started. It shows people you care and are committed.

As I expanded into other cities, I didn't always have time to meet with people face-to-face, but I did make it a point to take as many calls as I could.

I also tapped into my broader network letting them know what I was doing and asking for help. I'd send out an email newsletter once a quarter. I know that when I mention this newsletter technique, a lot of people are hesitant. They fear that they are "spamming" their friends.

Most people are willing to help out, and if someone feels like you're spamming them, they will let you know by unsubscribing. Don't take it personally. I just look at the unsubscribe rate of my email newsletter. If it's high, it's an indication that I've done something wrong.

I've taught this technique to a number of my students, and when they did it, they found out that their friends were actually curious to hear what they were up to and happy to help out any way they could.

Exercise 4.1: Reach out to your immediate network of close friends, family, and colleagues who you think are potential customers.

Objective: Leverage close relationships and turn them into customers.

Directions: Look through your existing network and reach out to people you think might be potential customers. You'll want to start by sending them an email.

Here's an example email I sent out to one of my early adopters:

Hi Linda,

It was great seeing you at yoga yesterday! As I mentioned in class, I am building a simple software solution to help independent studio owners like you get paid on time, keep track of students, and grow their business.

But before I dig into what I'm working on, I'd like to schedule a short meeting to understand the challenges you're facing with your business and see if there is an opportunity for me to help. Please let me know if you're available on: <dates>.

Looking forward to learning from you!

Kindly,
Poornima

- Notice that there is no obligation to buy anything.

- I've given a hint of what I'm building to get interest but just the core value proposition (no features).

Here's the follow up email requesting introductions:

Hi Linda,

Thanks again for taking the time to meet with me last week! During our conversation you mentioned that a few of your friends, Michele, Cynthia, and Jen, are also owners and instructors and might be willing to talk to me.

Would you mind doing an email introduction to them? I'd really appreciate it!

Kindly,
Poornima

Now create your email!

Exercise 4.2: Reach out to your larger network to let them know what you're working on and how they can help.

Objective: Leverage a larger network to help you spread the word and attract potential customers.

Directions: Craft an email and do the following in it:

- Keep the email short and to the point: 1-2 paragraphs max!

- Include one simple call-to-action (CTA) like: *"I'd really appreciate an introduction to any XYZ people you know."* Make it easy for them to follow through; I'd often give them a short blurb to pass on to people via email. The less time it takes, the more likely they are to follow through.

- Thank them for their time and help.

Section 3

Your initial audience will evolve

Hopefully by now I've convinced you why it's important to start talking to people and understand their needs before building or even talking about your idea!

And you're probably now wondering, *"How do I even find people to reach out to?"* *"What if they don't want to meet or are disinterested?"*

Three caveats before I dig into the specifics of building an audience:

1. **It's very likely that the type of customer you go after will change** as you're refining your idea. If that happens, then you'll need to do another round of conversations with the new set.

2. **Not everyone in your audience will become a customer.** Some will go on to become great referrals or influencers. Be open to opportunities and don't fixate on sales at this stage.

3. **You will face rejection.** There will be people who initially show interest but later become uninterested. Or you'll find that they are so busy that they cannot schedule a time to meet. Ultimately, it's up to you to move past rejection, find people who do have time, and persist through this process. You have to keep at it if you want feedback, and you need feedback before you can build!

But don't worry. If you follow the steps I've outlined below, you will be able to build an audience that is engaged and make use of that audience to conduct interviews, perform usability tests, and test out the prototype.

I'll be providing a number of strategies in this section, along with reasons why you should or shouldn't pursue a channel. Keep in mind that it does take time and a number of experiments to effectively build an audience.

Section 4

How to build an audience online

My 3 favorite online channels are Twitter, blogging, and email. I'm going to focus on just Twitter for now, but I'll dig into the others in the "Scrappy Marketing Strategies" chapter.

I have been a Twitter user since 2006, but honestly, I didn't really know how to use it for business purposes until the end of 2012!

The reason I think Twitter is a great channel is because it's an open platform. Yes, there are some people who protect their tweets, but the vast majority of people don't. You can freely follow people knowing who they are, where they are, and what they do.

People complain that there is no guarantee that people will follow you back, it's really hard to engage with anyone because you have to be pithy, and the real-time element means that you have a narrow window to attract folks. Those are all valid criticisms, but here's how you should be thinking about its usage:

- **Tweet consistently.** Twitter is a microblogging platform. That means you have 140 characters to convey a thought or message. Given the real-time nature, you cannot convey it just once and be done; you have to say it again and again, over different time windows and with varied content.

- **Reach out.** If you follow me on Twitter then you might notice that I'm constantly reaching out to people and asking questions or for feedback. Some of my followers respond immediately. Striking up the conversation is key. I also recommend taking the conversation off Twitter and into a longer form of messaging like email or a phone call.

- **Establishing common ground.** Not every single one of my followers cares about this guide—I know, hard to believe! I tweet about a variety of topics from startups to yoga to what I'm doing in the moment, like what dish I'm cooking for dinner or what book I'm currently reading.

- **Tell people to follow you.** If you want to build up your base of followers, it's not enough to just follow people and wait for them to follow you back. Be sure to include your Twitter handle in your marketing materials. I include my handle in all my presentation slide decks, in my email signature, and of course on my website.

- **Follow influencers and their followers.** If you have thought leaders in your space that you know people love to follow, follow their followers. Their followers are engaged and chances are if you are offering a product, service, or knowledge that is similar but slightly different from the influencer's, their followers will follow you back. The same rule applies to your competitors!

Following these steps will cause Twitter to take notice of your activity and recommend you to other people on their platform. This will help you continue to build your base of followers.

Exercise 4.3: If you haven't yet set up a Twitter account for your idea, do it now!

Objective: To start creating a presence on social media for your idea.

Directions:

- Include a professional image of yourself or your company's logo. Having the default Twitter egg as your image will leave people thinking your account is defunct.

- Put a brief description of what you are offering. Once again, this needs to be a high-level value proposition.

Exercise 4.4: Start following people on Twitter.

Objective: To start reaching out to people on social media, and build up an awareness about your idea.

Directions:

- Start following people whom you think might be potential customers.

- Wait for folks to follow you back, and don't feel bad about unfollowing people who don't follow you. I use Tweepi[23] to bulk unfollow people who haven't followed me back. Then I can go back to following new people.

- Use Twitter's search functionality to find folks to follow who meet the criteria of potential customers. For example, I often search for "yoga instructor" and "yoga studio owner" for BizeeBee. For Femgineer, I search for "software engineer," "software developer," "designer," "web designer," and "entrepreneur."

Exercise 4.5 Start tweeting!

Objective: Start engaging with your followers.

Directions:

- Tweeting in real time can be time-consuming. I often write and schedule my tweets a few days before they go live using a service like BufferApp,[24] which lets me set up time intervals for when they should go out. I can also use its analytics feature to gauge which tweets resonated with my audience. Then, a couple times a day, I'll check to see if anyone mentioned me using the @-reply.

- You can't just schedule your tweets and walk away, or else people will think you're just a robot. As I mentioned before, you do have to be engaged and have conversations with people. This can get time-consuming, so find some time in your schedule when you can engage with your followers.

Exercise 4.6 How to build an audience offline

People overlook offline channels because they're eager to get online and scale. But offline channels can be great at generating word of mouth as well because they give you a chance to meet people face to face.

Sometimes it's easier for people to reject you online, because they just don't know who you are! I've found that offline channels are the best way to dispel any myths or misconceptions people have about who I am and what my business does.

If you are concerned about scale, then I recommend finding places where big pockets of your customers might be hanging out.

Professional associations, clubs, meetups, and conferences are a great source of leads.

However, the heads of these groups don't appreciate people just coming in to solicit products. So if you want to show that you care and are authentic, consider joining and becoming a member or sponsoring an event if you can.

When I was looking for customers for BizeeBee, I'd write to people, but they either wouldn't respond or would come back with something like *"I'm not interested in buying software."*

I got tired of these responses, so I decided to start walking into yoga studios. When people saw me they didn't think, *"Oh, now there's someone trying to sell something!"* Instead they just saw a 5' 2" woman with a smiling face. I politely asked if I could have a minute of their time, and they were more willing to engage with me in person!

Most were open to chatting with me, but often times people are busy, so it's best to book some of their time in advance.

You can also reach out online and then insist on an offline meeting. This is exactly what one student in my email course, Quentin, did to attract customers to interview for his product BnBFlow[25]. BnBFlow helps AirBnB hosts manage post-book activities and logistics.

Quentin told me the following:

"This week I started to talk to fellow AirBnB users in order to validate the need for such a product. A meeting was organized by AirBnB in New York. 100 people, roughly, were invited.

I contacted a large number of them prior to the event and asked if they'd be open to a conversation about AirBnB management processes and a demo of the product, staying vague about what the product is doing, in order to have face-to-face encounters and the opportunity to talk directly with prospects.

I contacted 37 people (only power users with a large number of reviews). 17 told me they were interested in talking to me about the product."

Quentin identified an event where a large number of his prospective customers would be hanging out. He streamlined the list by seeking out power users and messaged them prior to the meeting.

While it's natural that not everyone would respond, nearly 50% did, and now Quentin has 17 people who have agreed to do an interview with him.

Review

It can be tempting to jump into building your product because you want to show prospective customers something visible or tangible. However, this limits the conversation, and you may discover that your product doesn't fit their needs. Instead of building and talking about your product, you'll want to understand what potential customers are going through. But, of course, you need customers to talk to! So start by building an audience. You can tap into your network, ask for referrals, and reach out to folks both online and offline. Once you've built out an audience, you can draw from this pool to conduct customer interviews, which is what we'll be covering the next chapter.

What you've validated in this chapter

If you completed the exercises, then you should have validated the following:

- There is an initial early audience (a subset of your broader target market) who may be interested in your idea.

- There are online and offline channels you can use to connect to this initial audience.

Chapter 5

Finding Your Customer Segment

The way the press and media tell the story behind Mint.com makes it seem like it all happened within two short years. In reality, Aaron Patzer, the founder, started working on it towards the end of 2005. I started collaborating with him then, and officially joined in the fall of 2006.

It took us 2 years to research and build the prototype. We launched in the fall of 2007 and were immediately faced with formidable competitors: Geezeo, Intuit, and Wesabe. Knowing this, we maintained our focus and kept refining the product.

At the end of 2009, Intuit acquired us.

I tell this story because it's easy for people to think that founders are somehow omniscient and customers just come flocking to them. However, this is simply not true. Entrepreneurs actually spend a fair amount of time doing research to identify potential customers and talking to them to develop a deep level of understanding.

Contrary to a popular belief that companies like Apple just know what customers want and build it, Jay Elliott's book *The Steve Jobs Way* walks readers through the elaborate process that Apple went through in order to understand its customers in the early days.

The initial process for understanding who your customers are is to take the time to discover who they *might* be. This is known as the customer discovery phase.

This is not the phase to approach people ad hoc, and it's not the stage to say, *"Tell me what you want and I'll build it,"* or even, *"Here's what I've built, will you pay me $X for it?"*

In Chapter 3, I covered the topic of market research and spoke about unearthing neglected segments. These are groups of people that your competitor has chosen not to service or may be unfamiliar with because they are new. You might have a hypothesis about these neglected segments. In order to validate that hypothesis, you've got to reach out, talk to people, and research their needs by interviewing them.

Before I dig into how to conduct interviews, I want to provide you with some motivation by explaining why this is a crucial step in building products that people will fall in love with.

By performing a customer interview, you can get clarity on a customer's problems and focus on building the right solution rather than jumping into building a prototype, only to discover later that customers don't want what you've built!

I know you might have already built a prototype and may not have talked to any customers yet. So I want to begin by sharing what one student, Renee, told me about what she and her team discovered when they went on-site to meet customers:

"Initially, we did brainstorming in-house and came up with a bunch of ideas. We decided to interview a group of customers and validate our ideas. But we were asked to follow the steps of the design thinking process and not jump to the ideation phase without the observation.

We went and observed the customers in their natural conditions before we started asking questions. I was very surprised that I learned a lot by observation as well, things that I did not think of before going to interview them.

We had more understanding of people's needs and a lot of insights to their actual lives. We threw all our initial ideas out of the window and came up with a great set of solutions which we felt confident were more valuable and would have an impact on them."

What's interesting here is that Renee and her team inserted an additional step, observing customers, and learned a lot even before asking questions! Of course she then went on to ask questions. Now Renee and her team are off in the right direction and can continue to refine their product idea.

Try to observe customers before the interview, and see if it deepens your understanding of them.

Section 1

Customers vs. early adopters

Too many people tell me they've contacted 5 to 100+ people, but the folks they contacted just weren't interested in their product. This ultimately causes them to conclude that there is no interest in the product.

However, when I do a deeper dive and ask them:

- *Whom did they contact? And to describe more about them, What is their persona? Not just something superficial like "women" or even "women in their thirties," but a really deep dive into their personal preferences in addition to external characteristics.*

- *Why was the person uninterested? Are they using a competing product? What are their main concerns with yours?*

People are often speechless.

The main problem here is that too often we target mainstream customers rather than *early adopters.*

An early adopter is someone who is interested in the product you have, either because they think it's a novel experience or will solve an acute pain they have. They are also willing to take a risk and try something new. This is the primary characteristic that differentiates them from mainstream customers.

Here are additional early adopter characteristics that you want to be on the lookout for. The early adopter often:

- Has a problem
- Is aware that they have a problem
- Is using substitutes (other products) or a workaround
- Is actively looking for a solution
- Has a budget

Contrast early adopters with *mainstream customers,* who mask their risk aversion and lack of interest by asking questions like:

- *"How long has the product been out in the market?" (They are verifying your product's credibility.)*
- *"Do you have XYZ feature?"*
- *"How much does it cost? Is there a discount?"*
- *"Who else is using the product?" (They want to see social proof.)*
- *"Can I have more time to make a decision?" (Indecision is still a decision and a sign of risk aversion.)*

These are all valid concerns and should be addressed eventually. But when you're just getting started, you cannot appeal to all their concerns. So you instead have to focus on targeting early adopters.

If you see the signs of risk adoption or lack of interest, you should temporarily walk away. You won't be able to convince them until later. Keep them updated on your progress, share testimonials, and let them know when you add features. But don't expect them to hand you any money as you get started.

Section 2

The perils of appealing to a wide customer base

Aside from going after mainstream customers, another issue that I come across is people who try to appeal to a really wide group (e.g., women in their thirties).

The reasoning is something like, "*Well, we don't want to exclude anyone.*"

Unfortunately, when you're just getting started you need to exclude as many people as you can. I know this seems counterproductive to the growth of your product, but here's why it's beneficial.

First, remember how I mentioned nuanced needs before? You cannot build for all of these nuanced needs initially. If you want to provide value, you have to narrow down your customer segment.

Second, remember back when I talked about *positioning*? When you are developing a position, you need to get as specific as possible. Otherwise, people won't understand whom the product is for. Many will dismiss it as being similar to a competitor's rather than take the time to understand how your product is different and whether it's for them. This type of thinking causes products to become commodities, and you'll notice that, too often, businesses end up competing on price alone.

It's perfectly OK to develop a strong position that makes it very clear whom your product is and isn't built for.

Think about it this way: do you want to service customers whose needs you absolutely know your product meets? Or, do you want to service customers who may be less than 100% satisfied and then go on to complain about how your product didn't meet their needs?

Probably the former.

Hence, your initial goal should be to develop a loyal following of early adopters whose needs you can meet. Then they will go on to spread the word about your product and act as reference customers. In order to cultivate this group, you have to start by narrowing down your customer segment, getting as specific as possible, and honing in on just 1-2 needs that you can meet. You'll discover those needs by conducting customer interviews.

Let's move on to laying a foundation for those interviews.

Section 3

Qualifying customers

The first thing I'm going to have you build is a qualification questionnaire. It is just a simple and small set of questions that you are going to use to qualify whether or not the person who is answering the questions is seeking a product and would be willing to participate in additional user studies, such as customer interviews, usability testing, and even become a paying early adopter.

This is an important first step because you don't want to waste someone's time if they're not willing to participate and provide useful feedback.

Too often, people skip this step and jump right into talking about the problem and product. However, this approach causes people to discover that the person they are talking to either doesn't care, doesn't have time, or doesn't experience a similar problem. (Recall Hermione's Hunch in the last chapter.) To avoid this situation and find the right set of customers, you want to take the time to create this qualification questionnaire. You'll be surprised at the quality of people you do get to participate in your customer and product development processes by using this technique.

Hopefully you've been building an audience based on the exercises I gave you in the previous chapter. One of the reasons I had you do this first is so that you can send this qualification questionnaire out to your audience. If you haven't built an audience yet, take a couple steps back and start to build one now. Otherwise, you won't have a good sample set to work with.

Once you've built your audience, you are going to send this qualification questionnaire out to that audience, much like you would send a survey. I know what you're thinking: "*Survey? Who answers those?*"

This is why you are casting a wide net. It's very likely that only about 1-2% will respond at all. Keep in mind that the goal is to get about 5-10 people who are pre-qualified in order to conduct some initial customer interviews.

To get 5-10 qualified leads, you need to send the qualification questionnaire out to about 1,000 people.

You can improve your results by sending it out to a smaller set of people, but in order to get enough qualified responses, you need to make sure your list is more targeted based on a detailed persona of your potential customer.

Section 4

Attracting additional audience groups

Keep in mind that while you might think there is a specific type of customer you are going after, there are a number of people who actually influence a customer and are actively involved in purchasing a product. These additional people are:

- Decision makers (people who make purchasing decisions within a group like a family or business)
- Economic buyers
- Recommenders
- Influencers

You'll want to make sure that you reach out to these people as well, because a number of them can provide a lot of insight regarding your customers. They also often act as strong influencers and may have a large network filled with potential customers for you.

For example, at Mint.com we reached out to a number of blogs like LifeHacker[26] because we figured its readers would be interested in learning how Mint.com could streamline their financial lives. We established the relationship before we launched, because we knew LifeHacker cared about its credibility and would want to see how we'd evolve as a service before recommending us to its readers. The initial post put out by LifeHacker did indeed pique the curiosity of its readers.[27]

Section 5

Create a qualification questionnaire

You want to make sure you have a good set of candidates you can use for interviews and usability tests. To recruit them you're going to create a qualification questionnaire. The qualification questionnaire should be no more than 5-7 questions. The first two questions should *qualify* the user, and the next ones should dig into the specifics of the problem.

Here's an example of a questionnaire that I created for BizeeBee:

1. **Do you currently own a yoga studio or manage one?** *I am mainly interested in talking to studio owners and managers, and no one else just yet.*

2. **Do you use a software program to manage your studio?** *I want to know if they are using a competitor's solution.*

3. **If you answered yes to #2, are you happy with your software program?** *If they are unhappy, then they may be looking for a better solution.*

4. **If you answered no to #2, why aren't you using a software program?** *If they hate software, then chances are they won't be early adopters. If they just hate what's out in the market, then they may be looking for a better solution.*

5. **Would you be interested in exploring a new software program to manage your studio?** *If they aren't interested then I don't want to waste their time or mine.*

Notice that I'm not getting into any details of my solution; I am merely determining whether they are interested and would be a good interview candidate.

Exercise 5.1: Create your own qualification questionnaire and send it out!

Objective: To recruit people who are actually interested in your idea, may be potential customers, and can help with various stages like customer interviews and usability testing.

Directions: Do not type these questions inside of an email and expect people to email you a reply back. People are lazy and hate to type; they'd prefer just clicking! Plus, you might not have everyone's email addresses and may need to post the questionnaire on other channels.

My two favorite products for creating forms are **Wufoo**[28] and **Google Forms**.[29] I love their forms because they are super easy to create and you can embed them into your website. This is especially important if you don't have people's email addresses and need to reach out to them via a tweet or a post. Embedding the form into a website gives it more context and credibility than if it's just a direct link within the tweet or post.

Pro tip: If you are going to embed the form on your site, make sure that the page you send them to doesn't have additional links like site navigation or unrelated CTAs (calls to action), such as buttons. This will distract people from filling out your form! Wufoo also gives you some great analytics, like how many people viewed the form and filled it out.

Now, take the link to your form and put it in a very short email—3 lines max!

Here's an example with a link; Google Forms also gives you the option to embed the form in the email:

Hi there,

I'm building a solution for yoga studios to manage their businesses, and I'd really appreciate it if you took just a moment to answer just 5 questions. Your feedback will help me build a better solution!

Answer questions now![30]

Kindly,
Poornima

You can also post the questionnaire link on your favorite social media channels. If you're sending it out in a tweet, do something like:

I'm looking to help yoga studios manage their business & need some feedback. Want to help? Please answer 5 questions http://buff.ly/1eoN55r

3 more important tips:

- **Get the survey respondents' contact info.** This is not a blind survey. You want to follow up with these people, so you'll need to include fields for their names and email addresses or some other contact info.

- **Add validation to the form elements.** People will inevitably fat-finger their email addresses or ramble on if you give them a text box (if you do, limit the number of characters). This is super easy to do with Wufoo, more so than with Google Forms. And be sure to indicate a field as "required" if you need respondents to answer a question.

- **Test your form out!** Go through the form once, answer the questions, and make sure the responses were recorded.

Pro tip: If you want to get fancy, you can also customize any email responses that go out once they've submitted the form. I find that

---

these personal touches keep people interested and engaged because you're showing your appreciation.

Once you've sent your qualification questionnaire out, you'll need to wait about 24-48 hours to get a response. Most people respond within that period of time. Some will take up to a week, but after that point, it's highly unlikely that they will respond.

If you send it out via email and don't get a single response within a week, then send a follow-up email with a friendly reminder. Don't feel like this is an intrusion; sometimes people just have a busy week, and there is no harm in sending them a short follow-up note.

If you sent the link out via social media, then people may miss it if they weren't around at the time you posted. So feel free to post it at a few different times during the course of a week.

If you still don't get any responses, then chances are you'll need to take an alternate approach like honing in on people from your network and reaching out to them. Or changing your messaging to help people understand why it's important for them to respond by explaining to them the end goal of what you're doing.

Following up

Once you do get responses, you need to take the time to identify the people who are qualified and follow up with them.

The next step is to do a customer interview, and I'll get into the specifics of how to conduct a customer interview in the upcoming sections.

The key to following up is to keep building engagement, and to do that, you're going to need to keep the momentum going. So contact the qualified person, thank them for filling out the questionnaire, and ask if they'd be open to doing a 30-60 minute interview either in person or online. Give them a few time slots when you're available, and if that doesn't work, then ask them what works for them.

You want to make the process as noninvasive to their schedule as possible, but you still want them to commit and be focused during the interview.

Don't wait more than a week to do the follow up! It's fine if it takes a few weeks before you have the interview.

If they don't respond, remember that people get busy, and don't hesitate to send out a friendly reminder!

For friendly reminders in general, I have a 1-2-3 rule. I follow up 1 week after my initial contact. If I haven't heard back, then I reach out again 2 weeks after the first friendly follow up. If I still don't hear back, then I'll wait another 3 weeks before I send a final follow up. If I still don't hear back, then I'll just move on because they're either too busy or uninterested.

Section 7

Getting over the fear of interviewing people

It's only natural to feel fear. After all, you're reaching out to someone with the risk that they'll reject you. If you do get the interview, then it can be a little bit scary to be in front of them. But here's the deal: they are actually more scared of YOU!

I know it seems weird.

Here's why: we are all taught to stay away from strangers as kids. So if someone reaches out and asks to interview us, we are going to be a little bit hesitant. We don't know who they are or what they want, and we are super busy; plus, they could be a psycho!

If you want to get over your fear, help others open up to you, and, most importantly, identify problems people are experiencing to validate your idea, then you've got to think in terms of just having a conversation with your closest friend.

That's all this is! Don't overthink it.

Exercise 5.2: Create your interview email.

Objective: Send out an email to set up a time to interview a potential customer.

Directions: Create a short email to send out to potential customers requesting an interview.

Here's what reaching out looks like as an email or letter:

Hi there,

I know you're super busy running your yoga studio, but I was wondering if I could stop by for a short visit. I'd like to learn how you manage your studio and hear about the problems you experience on a day-to-day basis.

Your insights would help me in building a solution to help yoga studios manage their business.

I know your time is valuable, so please let me know when you'd be available next.

Kindly,
Poornima

The shorter the better! Everyone is busy and has limited time, so get to the point of why you want to meet with them.

Once you get the meeting, you might fear sitting through 30 minutes or more with someone you don't know. So, right before you do an interview, you have to use a simple icebreaker. It will help calm yourself and the other person.

I like to start with the following: *"Thanks a lot for meeting with me, I really appreciate you taking time out of your day!"* Then: *"How's your day going?"*

Telling people you appreciate them shows you care! Ask them how their day is going is just polite, and gives them an opportunity to open up slowly.

Now create your email!

Section 8

How to conduct a customer interview

Hopefully by now I've provided you with sufficient reasoning and motivation to conduct a customer interview. So let's dig into how to do this!

If you've sent out the questionnaire and received results, the next phase is to look for the most promising interview candidates. You'll want to study their responses and see which ones said they'd be open to learning more and working with you.

I'd aim to do at least 5 initial in-depth customer interviews, but you may need to perform more if you don't have the right candidates or aren't seeing good results. For BizeeBee, I conducted 15+ face-to-face interviews with yoga studio owners before writing a single line of code!

I also want to warn you that you're actually going to be performing a series of interviews, not just one, as you continue to refine your product idea. In future lessons, I'll dig into how to perform usability tests using paper prototypes, interactive prototypes, and then a final prototype.

The common misconception is that we're conducting these interviews to confirm our idea. That is not the goal. Remember Hermione's Hunch? You want to avoid confirmation bias. Instead, you want to gain a deeper understanding of your customer. This understanding needs to go beyond surface-level problems.

Hence, in this initial stage, you do not want to talk about your product idea or solution. You want to get a deep understanding of the customer's needs and problems.

Exercise 5.3: Perform a customer interview.

Objective: Get a deep understanding of your potential customer segment to expose problems or needs they have.

Directions:

1. **Visit your interviewee onsite.** I always recommend meeting people onsite to help them feel more natural and "in their own habitat." Bringing them into your office makes them feel like they are really being interviewed, and the last thing you want is for someone to be stressed!

   When I conducted interviews for BizeeBee, I met yoga studio owners at their studios, and I learned a lot from being in their environment in addition to hearing their responses.

   It might not be possible for you to do this, and you might have to instead do a call or a remote interview via video chat. That's OK too, but I'd encourage you to visit if you have the means to make it happen, because you'll probably learn a lot from observing people in their settings, just like my student Renee did.

2. **Tell them what's going to happen.** You want to let them know how long the interview will last (usually 30-60 minutes) and whether they need to sign a release or waiver. You'll also want to mention that you will keep anything they tell you during the interview confidential.

   I recommend taking an audio or video recording, because I like to be engaging during the interview and keep the other person's attention (think Barbara Walters). So the last thing I want to be doing is taking notes. If you are going to do this, make sure the interviewer knows that you're recording and is OK with it. If they aren't, then you need to bring someone to take notes with you.

The other reason I recommend recording is that you can share the interview with teammates. It's much easier than handing them your handwritten notes, even if you have good handwriting, because it's hard to understand the context of a question and answer.

3. **Be present during the entire interview.** Remember, you are NOT going into the interview to validate your idea. Think about Hermione again: she walked out with results that were contrary to what she thought was the problem!

   You have to keep your personal biases aside and instead have a mindset of curiosity. People may convey behaviors that are odd to you. It's not your place to judge, only to know and understand that you'll need to consider these as you build your product.

4. **Ask different types of questions.** In the book *Interviewing Users*,[31] author Steve Portigal talks about the technique of asking naïve questions. For example, he'll walk in and ask someone, *"When is tax time?"* It might seem like a really obvious question to most, and you might feel like you're wasting someone's time asking them that, but the reason that you do this is to learn about their behaviors.

   Someone may respond with, *"I think it's April 15th, but I always file a month in advance."*

   It's great to know that's the behavior of one user, especially if you're creating tax software and trying to appeal to those who file early!

   I've also talked a lot about asking about people's pains and needs, but another important set of questions to ask are aspirational questions.

   For example, as we were conducting interviews for Mint.com, we'd ask people why they aspired to make more money. Surprisingly, not everyone had a greedy mindset. A lot of people said it would let them lead a fuller life. They could do things like take a trip to a far-off land or pay for their child's college tuition. Others said they'd love to donate to causes they believed in.

I got similar responses when I interviewed studio owners for BizeeBee and asked them what their goals were for starting a business. Many said they opened up their studio to be free from cubicle-land, and they really needed a system in place to help them achieve that goal!

You're asking aspirational questions to get a deeper understanding of your customers. That deeper understanding will eventually translate to product design and marketing materials.

5. **Tease out responses.** By now, you can tell that the responses you get are going to have some emotional weight to them, which is great! You want to note the language your subject is using and whether they are talking about positive or negative emotions.

Sometimes you might get an interviewee who is a little reluctant to share. This is why it's important to start each interview by establishing some rapport. It will help loosen them up a bit. Do an icebreaker and get to know them without coming off as invasive.

You may also get a flat or dead-end answer. In that case, it's OK to dig in a little bit deeper.

Back in 2010, I'd ask yoga studio owners, *"Do you use social media?"* Usually, they'd just respond yes or no. Some would be a little bit more emotional about it: *"Oh yes, I just LOVE Facebook,"* or *"Only for personal use."* Then I'd have to dig in a little bit deeper with a follow-up question like, *"Please tell me, why don't you use it for your business?"*

One time, someone responded, "I don't know how to set up a Twitter account." That was pretty telling! Even a tool like Twitter, which I might find easy to use, wasn't easy for some yoga studio owners back in 2010, which meant I'd have to build a product that was easier than Twitter.

Since some of you might be interested in creating products that automate people's tasks, you want to make sure people take the time to explain all the steps they perform, whether those are the steps in an ideal condition, and whether anyone else performs those steps. It's better if they show you so that you can see what they're doing, because sometimes an explanation can leave out key details that you may need to incorporate into your product's solution!

For example, I'd have yoga studio owners tell me all the steps that were involved with signing up a new student, but it wasn't until I saw them do it that I understood what was going on. It was eye-opening. There were a LOT of steps involved, and it would take anywhere between 1 to 10 minutes. Based on what I witnessed, I was able to create a simpler and more efficient workflow for them within BizeeBee that still helped them achieve the end goal of signing up a new student.

I call the initial interviews the "get-to-know you" phase. Your goal should be to establish enough rapport with potential customers so that you can do follow-up interviews.

In the initial interviews, you want to focus on behaviors, beliefs, and tasks. I advise against digging into specific products and even talking about the competition because you'll really limit the scope of the conversation. However, in subsequent interviews, you can get a little bit more product-centric.

6. **When you think you've dug deep, dig a little bit deeper.** When interviewing, too often people stop at surface-level sentiments. A surface-level sentiment might be something like, *"Oh, I hate the competitor's product."*

While this is great, it doesn't necessarily mean that they'll be willing to use yours. You have to dig in to understand what they hate about the competitor's product.

Basically, you are trying to understand their level of need. There are three types of needs, and once again, these are similar to characteristics of early adopters:

- Latent need: they have a problem and know they have a problem.
- Active need: they are actively searching for a solution.
- Vision: they have an idea for a solution and might have cobbled one together, but are prepared for a better one.

Here's a sample set of responses from an interview I conducted early on with BizeeBee to determine whether potential customers had a need for a new solution or were happy with the competitor's.

Me: If you don't mind me asking, why do you hate the competitor's solution?

Interviewee: *Because it's really hard to use, and it's clunky.*

Me: Why is it hard to use?

Interviewee: *Because it takes a long time to set up and you have to go through a number of steps to complete a single task like taking attendance.*

Me: Is there anything else?

Interviewee: *Yes. I have to pay to get trained on it, and I also have to pay to train my employees.*

Me: So you're concerned about the cost?

Interviewee: *Yes.*

Me: Why?

Interviewee: *Well, it's not so much the cost as it is about how much time it takes up. Time that could be spent with customers and doing sales. And even after the training, the product is still hard to use. There's just too much functionality in it. It takes a long time to learn.*

Me: What functionality do you not need? (And, I'd follow this up with questions about what they do need and whether they'd be willing to switch products to meet that need.)

Through this interview I was able to get some deep insights into why a customer felt the way they did about the competitor's product. This customer was clearly interested in making a switch. However, there are some customers who may show signs of interest but then have a level of loyalty to an existing solution that holds them back from trying something new.

This is characterized by things like brand affinity or how they think about the cost of switching, even though they might hate the other product!

Once again, this is a sign of a mainstream customer versus an early adopter.

I performed the first- and second-level interviews and listened to the customers' responses. From their responses, I was able to understand their needs and sentiments. Ultimately, this is the level of understanding you need in order to gain deep insights that can be translated into the design and marketing of a product.

Just as people fall in love with other people who get them and care for them, the same holds true for products. People fall in love with products that meet their needs. In order to fulfill a customer's needs, we need to know what they are, which is why we conduct customer interviews!

 ## Review

If you've jumped into building your product, I'd encourage you to take a step back. Remember, if your goal is to build a product that customers love, then you must have a deep understanding of your customer, and you need to find people who are in need of your solution. To do this in a way that is effective and efficient, start by creating a qualification questionnaire and sending it out to your audience. Using this questionnaire, you'll save time by finding a good set of prospective customers who are willing to take the time to work with you during your customer and product development processes. Follow up with those folks and schedule a customer interview with them. Go into the interview with curiosity and leave behind any biases that you may have. Remember: you are NOT your user!

Getting and conducting the interview may seem time consuming and daunting, but hopefully the case studies of students who have benefited from this approach will help you realize that you too will benefit from it.

What you've validated in this chapter

If you completed the exercises, then you should have validated the following:

- There is an initial early audience (a subset of your broader target market) who may be interested in your idea.
- There are online and offline channels you can use to connect to this initial audience.

How to Transform Your Ideas into Software Products

Chapter 6

Identifying Your Ideal Customer

People often ask me why I chose to work at Mint.com and how I knew we were going to be a success. Honestly, I didn't know if we would succeed. It was my first startup, so it's not like I had any prior experience "picking" winners. What I did know was that I had personally experienced the problem it aimed to solve. However, I was still concerned that I might be in the minority, and the product might only appeal to a tiny group of people.

It wasn't until the 10th person told me that Mint was a much-needed solution that I felt we were onto something. But this early positive sentiment still wasn't enough to make us build. We were hearing some varying feedback. People had nuanced needs, and we needed to hone in on what they really wanted.

You might be feeling the same way. If you've talked to at least one customer, you probably feel like you have some deeper insights into the customer than you did before, but it's not quite time to draw conclusions from your interview data yet.

First, you'll have to go broad and interview many people until patterns of needs emerge, allowing you to imagine distinct user personas with unique, nuanced problems. Once you have a true understanding of these potential customers' needs, you will be able to empathize with them, narrow down, and choose which segment to focus on first as you build your initial solution.

Section 1

Sample size skew

Interviewing one customer will only give you one person's opinion and views. Since we want to build for multiple people, we need to spot patterns, and in order to spot patterns, we need a large sample size of interview data.

I'm not going to tell you an exact number of people to interview. I will say that if you have interviewed fewer than 20 people and the results are all over the place, then you need to interview more until you start to hear similar problems and pain points.

Yes, I know that seems like a lot of interviewees, but remember that the goal is to build a product that many people will love! In order to do that, you must validate your hypothesis that multiple people have the same pain points and would want to experience similar benefits. Otherwise, you'll end up building a product that only one person loves.

Also, if you've already received exceptionally positive or negative feedback from a small sample size, you'll want to explore a little bit further. It's very likely that you've hit a niche group, which is great; they might even be your early adopters. But once again, you want to make sure that a small group doesn't color your knowledge of the issues that people face as it relates to the problem you are trying to solve.

So take the time to do some broad research. It's totally OK to have a few outliers, and maybe you'll expose some user segments that you could eventually target or expand to service.

Section 2

How to broaden your customer interview base

During your very first interviews, it's important that you find out how potential customers hear about products and services so that you can tap into those channels for more interviewees. Plus, in the future, knowing and engaging with people who frequent those channels will help you grow your audience.

When I interviewed the initial group of people for BizeeBee, I found out that many studio owners learned the most from talking to their friends who are also owners. So I learned that referrals would be key and made sure to ask for as many introductions as people were willing to make.

Another group I interviewed mentioned that they search online for solutions, but back in 2010, when I was conducting these interviews, hardly anyone mentioned using social media! That has changed dramatically. Customers are more receptive to it now. I had to keep my ear to the ground and understand what channels appealed to my customers and how their preferences evolved over time.

Of course, one could argue that the people who aren't using online channels aren't necessarily early adopters for software products. My response would be that is partially true. Some folks aren't using online channels because they don't know how to or might be too busy for online research. But they might still have a problem that can be solved with software! Don't make assumptions until you've talked to people, and interview potential customers even if they aren't using online channels.

And yes, it's true that a majority of early adopters will be online. To find those folks, you need to get online too! Post to online forums and let people know that you need help via social media channels.

If you're still struggling with recruiting interview candidates, then you'll need to continue to reach out to people in your network and ask for additional referrals.

Condensing interview feedback

Now, assuming that you've gotten a large enough sample size and interviewed them using the techniques from Chapter 5 (I interviewed about 25 yoga studio owners and instructors for BizeeBee around the country), it's time to sit down, review everything people said, and create behavioral descriptions of customers.

The goal of creating these descriptions is to gain clarity about whom you are building for and servicing.

If, during your interviews, you focused on listening to people and dug into their thinking, then you should have deeper understanding of what they are doing, which includes what they are doing when they aren't using a tool (software). You should have also gained an understanding of why they are doing those actions. If you don't, then you'll need to go back and ask them why.

It's crucial to have an understanding of their behaviors, because those are the behaviors that they have grown accustomed to. The "why" is also important because it associates their beliefs with their behaviors.

When you gain an understanding of their beliefs, then you'll understand what value they're looking for. Delivering value is what creates loyalty and prevents your product from being thought of as a commodity.

Ultimately, a customer's thinking and reasoning is what leads to their behaviors and the behaviors can be grouped into personas.

A user persona is a representation of the goals and behavior of a hypothesized group of users. In most cases, personas are synthesized from data collected from interviews with users. They are captured in 1- to 2-page descriptions that include behavior patterns, goals, skills, attitudes, and environments, with a few fictional personal details to make the persona a realistic character. For each product, more than one persona is usually created, but one persona should always be the primary focus for the design.[32]

In Indi Young's book *Mental Models*, Young says that in order to design a product that is going to resonate with people, you need to understand the behaviors for each persona. By doing so, you will experience the following benefits:

- **Confidence in your design**: guide the design of the solution.

- **Clarity in direction**: make good user and business decisions.

- **Continuity of strategy**: ensure longevity of vision and opportunity.

In Chapter 7, I'll dig into how to utilize the personas to guide your product's design. For now, I want to walk you through how to first create behavior descriptions and user personas from those descriptions.

Here are a few examples of potential customers and their behavioral descriptions I created from my BizeeBee interviews:

- A yoga business owner who runs their business from a single shared space such as a community center, because they believe a studio space is a lot of overhead to manage. Wants to use social media but struggles to understand how to use it to drive sales, so they instead talk to customers face to face. Knows that they need to get with the times and stop running their business off of index cards, but is concerned about the time it will take to get set up. Believes they are losing money because they are using index cards.

- A personal trainer who is just getting their business off the ground. Rents space at gyms to train clients. Believes that spending more time with clients will lead to a more profitable business. Doesn't always keep good records but believes that they should.

- A yoga instructor who teaches on-the-go at corporations and studios. They love teaching and believe that they should be spending the vast majority of their time teaching, not running their business.

- A studio owner who has owned their business for more than a few years and is looking to expand. Has hired help to offer high touch to customers. Believes that they need a system in place in order to grow, and keep records electronically.

Are you starting to see any patterns here in terms of behaviors and beliefs?

Let's take a closer look. The first 3 don't own a studio and have much smaller businesses than the fourth. However, they all believe that spending time with customers is how they will grow their business. Some believe that record keeping is a sound business practice.

From this we'll create three personas:

- **Small business owner who likes being small.** The business owner who doesn't have a physical space for their business and may be operating on-the-go or in a shared space. Keeps records of customers.

- **Small business owner who believes more in sharing their practice than building a business.** The business owner who believes they should be spending time with customers, not keeping records or running their business.

- **Small business owner who eventually wants to make it big.** The studio owner who owns space and may be looking to expand into another location. Believes in keeping records of customers.

At this stage, you might be tempted to pick a persona and start building for it. But you actually need to dig a little bit deeper in order to know what to build for your ideal customer. So sit tight for a little bit longer!

Exercise 6.1 Identify behaviors and create personas.

Objective: Identify beliefs that people hold, the behaviors that result from those beliefs, and then create personas.

Directions:

1. List out everyone you interviewed using the BizeeBee example above.

2. Identify the beliefs and the behaviors that emerge from it. If possible, highlight their beliefs using their own words. The easiest way to do this is to start by telling a story about who each interviewee is.

3. Look for common patterns in their needs, behaviors, and beliefs, then condense the patterns into 1-3 personas. Make a note of all the outliers.

4. Come up with a label for a persona and be sure to describe what it means.

Case Study

Botching BizeeBee's beta by going broad

Remember back in Chapter 1, when I mentioned why I decided to narrow my user segment? Well, I want to provide you with a little more context for why I went broad initially, and hopefully you'll learn from my mistake.

Back in 2010, I initially wanted to build a product that would appeal to yoga studio owners, so I set off to do a lot of customer research. As I was doing my research and discussing the idea with my startup-founder friends, some of them convinced me that it was just too small a market. They said, *"You should be thinking bigger!"*

I thought they knew something that I didn't, so I changed my approach and decided to target all small business owners.

I cast a wide net and interviewed a number of them, discovering that they experienced a common problem: cash flow management.

Between May 2010 and August 2010, my team and I set out to build a simple solution to manage cash flow and launched it as an alpha version the first week in August.

The day of the launch, we had hundreds of people log in and check out the product. I was really excited!

The next day, I noticed that no one came back. About a week went by and I started to get a little worried, but I waited one more week. Still, only silence.

I picked up the phone and started to call customers. When I asked them why they weren't returning, they said the following:

"I sell products, and this seems to be a great solution for those selling services."

"I sell services, but I really need a way to track time in addition to cash flow."

The conversations continued like this. Each small business owner told me about some nuanced need that I hadn't met.

Finally, I decided to scrap the entire product and start again, focusing on yoga studio owners. Between September 2010 and December 2010, my team and I built a solution just for independent yoga studio owners who exhibited the following characteristics:

- Were either newly opened, about to open, or didn't use any existing software solutions

- Wanted a super simple tool to grow their business

- Had less than $100K in annual revenue

- Had fewer than 30 students a class

- Had fewer than 2 staff members

Based on these characteristics, we were able to attract three early adopters. It might not seem like much, but one of them went on to be a customer for a year and another for nearly three!

Let's talk about how we can get you there by focusing on one ideal customer segment.

Exercise 6.2: Identify your ideal customer by getting into their character.

Objective: Choose which persona you'll build your initial solution for by observing which one you empathize with most.

Directions: If you can find a partner to do this exercise with, it will work well. If not, then record the conversation and play it back.

1. Pretend you are one person you'd like to help, and use first-person language: *"I'm Linda and I teach yoga."* If you are your own customer, you'll still need to leave aside your personal beliefs and interests because understanding other people's needs is important too.

2. Describe out loud who you are, where you live, and your interests, aspirations, and pains.

3. List out any limiting beliefs you have about goals, and why you may have them.

4. Now listen to the recording or have your partner repeat what you said.

5. Ask yourself: Is this type of person I'd like to help?

6. If you answered no, then pick another persona. If you're not sure, then you might need to do some more interviews to understand this persona better. And if you answered yes, then this is the segment you want to target, but keep in mind that you'll need to transcend their limiting beliefs!

The purpose of doing this exercise is to disconnect with your product idea, discover and understand your ideal customer persona, and become motivated enough to solve a problem for them.

Finding your ideal customer doesn't mean you cannot service other customer personas. But you must have "customer clarity" in order to guide your product decisions and marketing messages when you're just getting started. The clearer you are about whom you're serving, the easier it will be to attract a group of early adopters.

Review

Remember, if your goal is to build a product that customers love, you've got to make sure that you have a large sample size of interviewees. If you don't start seeing common patterns in your interview results, then you need to get out and interview more folks! Once you've conducted enough interviews, describe the user personas and the mental models behind them. Finally, narrow down and discover which persona is your ideal customer by stepping into each one's shoes and detecting which one you empathize with most.

What you've validated in this chapter

If you completed the exercises, then you should have validated the following:

- There are beliefs that lead potential customers to have certain behaviors.

- There are patterns among these potential customers that can be grouped into personas.

- There is an ideal customer that you'd like to initially focus on, and this focus is based on a deep understanding of who they are and what their needs are.

Chapter 7

Differentiating with Design

At the end of last year, my best friend, Jessica, got engaged to her longtime boyfriend, Ben. Since I do a lot of public speaking, she requested that I officiate the wedding. I was honored to accept, but I had never officiated a wedding before.

I remembered a couple of my friends mentioning that they had officiated weddings, and in order to get authorization, they just went online and filled out some documents. So, I did a couple searches and came across the Universal Life Church, which was highly rated and had some seemingly reputable testimonials.

I sat down one Saturday afternoon and signed up to be an officiant. The whole process took only a few minutes. It seemed too short. I'd been used to official processes that required hours of wait time, multiple documents, and a countless number of steps. I was immediately worried and thought, *"How could something like marrying two people only take a few minutes?"*

To double check, I emailed a friend who had officiated before, and they confirmed: "Yes, it is that easy."

Whew!

While the process seemed too simple, its simplicity made my life easy and helped me accomplish my goal: *to become an officiant.*

Accomplishing goals and feeling great is the exact outcome we want users to experience so that they fall in love with our software products!

The Universal Life Church is a prime example of a company that has done a great job designing a simple experience for its users. As a result, it has millions of users who have become officiants within minutes online.

If the Universal Life Church didn't exist, I'd probably have to fill out a lot of paperwork or even become a minister in order officiate my friends' wedding!

Figure 7.1 Officiating Jessica & Ben's wedding.

Section 1

Using design to get a competitive edge

In Chapter 3, I talked about the concept of positioning. Positioning is the process of creating an image or identity in the customer's mind. I also mentioned that you can position based on a number of factors: price, packaging, promotion, distribution, and competition.

In this chapter, I'm going to dig into positioning based on packaging, a.k.a. design. We'll talk about how to create a user-friendly product design that helps users reach their goals easily, just like the Universal Life Church did.

Now, I don't want you to worry about how to start designing your product just yet. We'll dig into the how-to in later sections, and I'll provide you with some techniques. For now, I'm going to give you an overview of how design can be used to gain a competitive edge, and I'll highlight a couple simple concepts that you can eventually incorporate into the design of your product.

Section 2

History of product design as competitive differentiation

In the '90s and early 2000s, people were building products that were really feature rich. Somehow, engineers and product managers were taught to believe that piling on features meant that the product was really robust, which would translate to more sales.

What it actually did was require users to read verbose manuals to understand how to use the product; or, it required them to pay for training. This, of course, assumed that users had the time, budget, and patience. For a good period of time, companies were able to get away with selling complicated products because there weren't many people putting software products on the market.

However, companies can no longer get away with this approach. The clunky products of the early Internet and shrink-wrapped software era have most recently been outdone by much simpler products entering the market—ones that have just a sliver of the features of their bloated predecessors.

Why?

Because people now have simple alternatives to choose from! As a result, they have grown extremely frustrated with feature-rich products and have decided that it's a waste of time to learn how to use these products. Now, customers demand tools that are intuitive and easily navigable.

Both my startups, Mint.com and BizeeBee, were based on the idea that people are time-starved and want a simple software solution to perform complex tasks like managing their personal finances or their small businesses.

Case Study

Differentiating Mint.com by building a dead-simple user experience

Mint.com was born out of a growing frustration that the founder, Aaron Patzer, had with existing software products like Quicken and Microsoft Money. It took Aaron hours each weekend to download transactions from his financial accounts and categorize them in order to finally achieve his end goal: knowing how much money he really had.

One of the goals of software is to automate complex tasks, but products like Quicken and Money weren't doing a good job of automating the process of managing money.

Even getting set up on these products took hours!

After one exceptionally aggravating Sunday, Aaron decided enough was enough! He'd take matters into his own hands and build a simpler solution to manage his personal finances.

From the beginning, we knew design would be one of Mint's positioning tactics. We designed every part to be as simple to use as possible, starting with getting set up. Mint connects to a user's financial institutions, then automatically downloads and categorizes the financial transactions. It only takes a few minutes and very minimal input from a user for them to see how much money they have.

Case Study

How Olark gained market share by making customer setup a cinch

Olark[33] is a startup that makes a live chat product for online and e-commerce businesses, helping them improve sales and handle customer support. Just like with Mint.com, getting set up with Olark is pretty simple. There is just one snippet of code that people need to cut and paste in order to embed the widget on their websites.

The chat widget looks like Google Chat. Some might consider this a rip-off, but it's actually taking advantage of the familiarity people have with another credible and highly used product. If the experience is familiar, then people will instinctively think this product is as easy to use as the other and are more likely to adopt it.

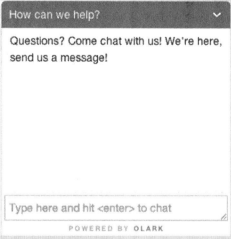

Figure 7.2 The Olark live chat widget.

While there are a number of other live chat products on the market, they're difficult to use. Even something as simple as connecting to another human being can take minutes, lead you through a number of redirect loops, and require you to provide a lot of information before you can start chatting.

With Olark, you get a pretty simple and elegant popup at the bottom of your website that customers can access anywhere.

Olark also makes it super simple for operators (people who are answering chat messages) to respond and keep track of conversations between customers easily.

The company focused on making their product as easy to set up as possible for anyone who wants to have live chat on their site. This not only increased its adoption rate, but also increased its number of paying customers.

What is UI/UX?

Over the years, people have become obsessed with UI (user interface) and UX (user experience), especially when it comes to web or mobile products. User interface is what a user sees, and user experience refers to how a user is able to move through the product and accomplish tasks.

In order to design a product that has good UI/UX, you need to understand the following two concepts: *information architecture and workflows.*

Information architecture is how information is organized, whether it's in a hierarchy or packaged in way that helps people make decisions. This is especially important in data-rich applications like Mint.com. Just spitting out a bunch of data would have really pissed users off and wouldn't have been much different from just logging into a bank or credit card account.

Instead, Mint.com takes transactions across a number of accounts (banks, credit cards, student loans, etc.) and then automatically creates "pretty pie charts" that have aggregated all the transaction data into categories like food, rent, etc.

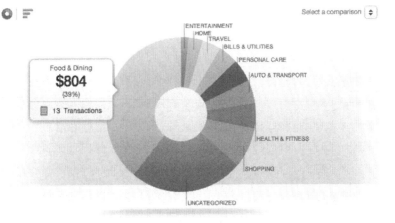

Figure 7.3 Mint's graph to represent spending.

Presenting data in this way lets people get a big picture of what's going on. Then, they can drill down further to understand their spending habits and maybe even decide to change them.

The most important thing to realize is that Mint takes the time to design how the data will be represented by understanding the end goal of its users: *to see where their money went.*

Too often, people think that the product just needs to be pretty. Aesthetics are important, but what's really important is that the product is functional (i.e., helps a user perform a task and ultimately accomplish a high-level goal).

Creating hierarchies of information in terms of importance or relevance is one way to help users accomplish goals by presenting the key information they need to make high-level decisions.

When it comes to information architecture, a good product designer will focus on making sure the data can be inputted into the product seamlessly. The designer makes sure information is kept clean, is organized, and is presented in such a way that makes it easy to make decisions.

Workflows are essentially the steps that people need to perform in order to accomplish a task. Most of the time, people think products are hard to use or unintuitive because of poorly designed workflows. If you've ever signed up for a product and then asked yourself the question, *"Now what?"* it means that no one took the time to think through the onboarding workflow for you.

Onboarding a user is an extremely critical workflow, because it is essentially a user's first impression of your product. If their first impression is, *"This looks complicated,"* or *"This is going to take time to set up,"* then chances are they won't come back after signing up and will look for a simpler solution.

The same is true for other features. If, as a user, you're just expected to "figure it out" or have an endless list of steps to perform, then someone hasn't done their job of making the product user-friendly.

Does it seem like this is quite a lot to do and think about when designing a product? Well, remember our end goal: *building a product that customers will fall in love with and pay for!*

If we want to accomplish that goal, then we have to make customers feel good as they are using our product, which means that they need to have positive experiences each time they use it.

However, I don't want you to conflate positive experience with *perfection.* This can be a treacherous path that rarely leads to shipping a product. I'll dig into how you can combat this thinking and ship a simple product that benefits customers.

Exercise 7.1: Critique competitors' product designs.

Objective: Spot design-related issues in your competitors' products as you look at onboarding workflows, general usage workflows, information architecture, and even aesthetic. Understanding your competitors' UI/UX weaknesses will help you design a better product.

Directions: Take a look at 3 competing products and answer the following questions:

1. How long does it take to sign up and get set up? Are all these steps necessary and easy to follow for a first-time user?

2. Based on your first interaction with the product, did you experience the benefits the company publicized? Or, do you feel like it will require more work on your part to receive value?

3. As you moved through the product, what did you find particularly helpful or confusing?

If there isn't a competing product or service to examine, then consider substitutes that people might be using. For example, at BizeeBee, a number of studio owners I met with showed me how they were managing their businesses on paper, index cards, or Excel. I'd have them walk me through their workflows so that I could get a deep understanding of the steps and processes they went through to keep track of customers and manage their businesses.

Hopefully I've provided you with enough motivation to take design seriously. Now, let's move on to how we're going to design your product.

Using interview data to guide your design

Remember how I had you condense your interview data and come up with behavioral descriptions and personas?

We're going to revisit those and identify a list of high-level verbs, or actions, that each persona performs.

For example, here are the personas I created for BizeeBee:

- **Small business owner who likes being small.** The business owner who doesn't have a physical space for their business and may be operating on-the-go or in a shared space. Keeps records of customers.

- **Small business owner who believes more in sharing their practice than building a business.** The business owner who believes they should be spending time with customers, not keeping records or running their business.

- **Small business owner who eventually wants to make it big.** The studio owner who owns space and may be looking to expand into another location. Believes in keeping records of customers.

Combing through the interview transcripts, I spotted the following verbs for each persona:

Independent yoga studio owner verbs:

- **Teach** yoga class
- **Take** attendance
- **Schedule** instructors
- **Ask** students for payments

- **Track** studio's income

- **Own** or **manage** a studio

- **Perform back office tasks** (Or, a business partner does this.)

Yoga instructor verbs:

- **Teach** yoga class 1-1

- **Teach** yoga classes at a studio

- **Teach** yoga classes in corporations

- May **teach** full time or part-time

- **Take** attendance

- **Ask** students for payments

- **Travel** to teach

- **Track** personal income

The next step is to use these two lists to do the following for each persona:

1. List the distinguishing behaviors

2. Group the common behaviors

We want to design for as many of the common behaviors as we can and validate whether those are enough to appeal to both segments. If they aren't, then we'll need to focus on just one persona to avoid complicating our design and confusing our users.

Here are the common behaviors across the two personas:

- **Teach** yoga classes at a studio

- **Take** attendance

- **Ask** for payment

The next step is to search for **tasks** in the interview data. Tasks are the steps that customers perform in relation to a high-level behavior (i.e., the verbs identified in the previous steps). The tasks are what you'll go on to emulate in your product's design, and you'll create workflows for them.

However, remember that you have limited resources! You can't emulate every single task, and it might not be necessary to attract an early adopter. You'll want to understand a customer's desires, feelings, preferences, and expectations in relation to each task. This will characterize their level of need, and based on their level of need, we can prioritize what to build!

To evaluate tasks, we need to reference quotes from the interview. Here are a couple examples:

- *"Every class, students come in and we need to check them in. As we check them in, we see if their membership is still valid or expired. If it is expired, we need them to renew their membership. If we don't do this, then we lose money on expired memberships, and we're basically giving away classes for free."* (This is an important task and translates back to the business staying solvent!)

- *"My front desk person checks students in."* (There are multiple people performing this task.)

- *"Taking attendance should be fast and easy."* (A strong preference.)

- *"I don't like asking students for money right when they check in."* (A strong preference.)

- *"I wish students would just pre-pay for classes and their memberships."* (A strong desire.)

- *"I think students will pre-pay for classes and memberships if it's convenient."* (An expectation.)

Based on these quotes, we can start to get a sense of the customers' goals.

Next, we can list the overarching tasks associated with each of these quotes:

- Enter student info

- Take attendance

- Review attendance

- Collect payment and record membership

- Review expired memberships

- Notify students whose memberships have expired

We need to understand whether there are pauses between these tasks, whether they are performed in chronological order, and how the data flows through each of them.

So, we model the task flow:

1. Enter student info   2. Take attendance   3. Review attendance

Then, we identify the data needed between each step:

- Between steps 1 and 2, we need: student info, purchase data, expiration date of purchase.

- Between steps 2 and 3, we need: class info and student attendance.

Once you've identified the tasks, you might want to jump into creating wireframes, but there are still two more steps.

First, take a task and translate it into a **user story**. A user story is a way of representing the task that a user performs, along with the goal that drives it. User stories serve as the common unit that engineers, product managers, and designers reference when they are talking about what is going to be built, how it will function, and the end result.

The format for a user story is: *persona + task + goal.*

Here's an example of a user story:

As a yoga studio owner, I'd like to **take attendance** *as students check in to class, in order to keep memberships up-to-date.*

A set of stories feeds into a feature.

Let's say we know that we need to create a high-level feature called "account creation." We'll then need to create a set of stories around that feature, and they might be something like:

As a yoga studio owner, I'd like to create an account on BizeeBee, to keep my business organized.

As a yoga studio owner, I need to first create a username and password, in order to create an account on BizeeBee.

As a yoga studio owner, I need to create a unique username, in order to avoid conflicting with another yoga studio owner's account.

As a yoga studio owner, I need to create a strong password, in order for my password to be secure.

You'll notice that there are a number of stories that fit into a feature, and they are pretty granular. For now, just know that this is necessary; in an upcoming chapter I'll explain why. Hopefully, you're starting to see how all this work is coming together!

Exercise 7.2: Discover common tasks and create user stories.

Objective: Identify common user workflows that you'll want your product to automate.

Directions:

1. Comb through the interview data and spot common verbs.

2. Next, list out all the tasks associated with each verb.

3. Group the common behaviors across personas and make a list of the ones that are different.

4. Look for customer interview quotes that will give you a better sense of the tasks that are the most important and the goals associated with those tasks.

5. Create user stories using the following formula: *persona + task + goal.*

Exercise 7.3: Create a storyboard of your customer's experience with your product.

Storyboarding your customer's experience will help you ensure that your product actually *works* well before you start thinking about what it *looks* like.

Objectives:

1. For each user story you created in the previous exercise (Exercise 7.2), you're going to identify the steps the user will take through your product to accomplish the goal.

2. Learn how to simulate positive and negative scenarios (error conditions).

3. Demonstrate how every step of the product supports the user in completing the goal in the user story.

---

4. Craft narratives using actual customers' names that can be referred to throughout the whole product development process.

5. Go beyond the user stories and consider the customer's environment, emotions, needs, and outcomes.

6. Foster collaboration within your team by using low-fidelity collaboration tools (sketching, whiteboard, etc.)

Directions:

1. Start by creating a storyboard template by dividing a page into 8 boxes. You'll do this for each user story you listed in Exercise 7.2, so you'll need 1 page for each user story. Be sure to give each person a name and indicate their states of mind, needs, and desires on their page.

2. For each user, fill in the boxes sequentially with each small interaction they make with your product.

3. Next, go back through the boxes and draw very rough screens indicating what the key call to action is for each step.

4. Next, use lines to show how various steps or scenes of the story interact with other steps.

5. Finally, verbally talk through the entire storyboard with at least two people. Under each box on the storyboard, indicate the main purpose of that step along with any concerns, learnings, or important things to keep in mind.

Section 5

The power of paper prototyping

In early 2014, I hosted a Femgineer Forum[34] in San Francisco. As I was packing up to leave, one of the attendees, Renee, asked if she could bum a ride with me, and I happily obliged.

During our drive, Renee and I got to talking. She told me that she recently received a promotion at her job, which pleased her, but she was left wondering, *"What next?"*

Climbing the corporate ladder was not the direction she wanted to take her career in, and while she had a lot of ideas and knew that she was capable of building a software product on her own, she was just not sure she wanted to take a bunch of time to build something that people might not be interested in. Plus, she had very limited time to build anything given that she had a full-time job!

You might feel the same way as Renee: *Why spend countless hours coding to build something people may not want?*

Or, you might be someone who is eager to build something to show to customers, thinking that it's the only way people will provide you with valuable feedback.

Well, I'm here to offer a different approach.

I advise both technical and non-technical founders not to build anything until they have validated their product design on paper. Yup, that's right—paper!

Yes, I know, it seems a bit crazy, but that's actually what I did with my startup, BizeeBee.

For the first six months, I didn't build a damn thing, even though I knew how to code! Truth is I'm lazy when it comes to coding. I only want to code things that I know people want and will pay for. So, I did a lot of customer interviews and then followed up with usability tests based on paper prototypes. You can actually receive a ton of validation and valuable feedback from doing a usability test on paper.

You're probably skeptical. I can assure you that every single student I've taught, from my Lean Product Development Course to students at Duke University, created a paper prototype first and got valuable feedback from customers! They ended up thanking me because they were able to iterate quickly on paper and build the *right features* into their products.

To create paper prototypes for our usability tests, we first need to create wireframes. A **wireframe** is a simple blueprint that represents your product.

- The kinds of information displayed
- The range of functions available
- The relative priorities of the information and functions
- The rules for displaying certain kinds of information
- The effect of different scenarios on the display[35]

We create wireframes to:

- start a conversation with customers
- clarify purpose and value
- visualize the product
- test general flows
- test information, navigation, and interface

As you're designing your wireframes, you want to answer the following questions:

- What are the common workflows a customer is going to perform?

- What is the set of data they will need in order to perform each workflow?
- How will the data exist in the system? Will it be pulled in automatically, or will the customer need to input it ahead of time? If it's the latter, there may be additional workflows the customer needs to undergo.

Once again, let's use BizeeBee as an example.

You'll notice that in order to take attendance for a yoga studio member, I'll need to see whether the member exists. If they don't, I'll need to add the member before taking attendance.

Exercise 7.4: Create a paper prototype of your product and perform a usability test.

Objectives: Gain feedback on product workflows and validate whether the design addresses customer needs.

Directions:

1. **Create a paper prototype.** Draw a paper prototype with wireframes based on the storyboards you created in Exercise 7.3. Feel free to create 3-5

Figure 7.4 BizeeBee paper prototype home screen

---

prototypes if your storyboards vary. For more guidance, you can check out a talk I gave at Startup Product Summit called **Validate Your Product on Paper.**[36] I've also made the slides available.[37] If you want to learn even more about the power of paper prototyping, check out the book *Paper Prototyping* by Carolyn Snyder.

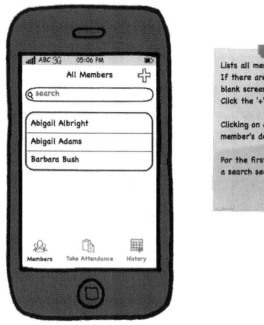

Figure 7.5 BizeeBee paper prototype add members.

2. **Schedule a usability test.** Just as I had you schedule customer interviews back in Chapter 5, you are going to schedule time to meet with customers yet again, this time for usability tests. Try to use the same group of customers, because continuity of feedback is useful. Plus, your customers will be thrilled to see you progress and start to become invested in the product.

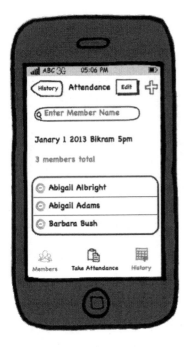
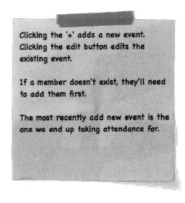

Figure 7.6 BizeeBee paper prototype take attendance

3. **Ask permission to record the usability test.** Recording will help you see how people moved through the product and share that with your teammates.

4. **When you meet, you'll want to set people's expectations.** Start by letting them know that you are not testing them, but that you are testing the product. Have them walk through the product and as they are interacting with it, simulate the behavior. Hold off on asking them any questions while they are interacting with the paper prototype. But do let them know that they should ask questions if they are confused. I used to recommend having the customer think out loud, but have received mixed results.

5. **At the end, ask people for feedback** on what was confusing and what was clear. Finally, ask them if the prototype

contains the benefits they are looking for, or if they were expecting something else.

Do these usability tests live, if possible. If you cannot find locals to meet in person, you can also use a service like UserTesting.com to automate the process of usability testing. However, I highly recommend doing at least a handful of in-person usability tests. Watching people interact with your product, even on paper, will really help you understand what works and what needs work!

In case you don't want the guilt of killing trees on your conscience, paper prototype responsibly by recycling.

Section 6

Stages of usability testing

Don't be afraid to iterate on the paper design a few times and get many customers to review it. You want to feel confident and get validation at this early stage before you move on to creating more refined prototypes.

Performing a usability test on paper is just the first stage; there are at least 3 more prototyping stages I highly recommend.

The second stage is taking your paper prototype and making it interactive! You can make a clickable prototype using Balsamiq[38] or InvisionApp[39]. The goal, again, is to test workflows. In the following exercise, you'll create an interactive virtual prototype.

In the third phase, you're going to produce a **high-fidelity mockup**. A high-fidelity mockup is essentially a Photoshop file. It's what your product will eventually look like. This is the point where you'll start to test things like color, look, and feel. You can perform a usability test by printing these out on paper, or you can skip ahead to making an interactive mock using InvisionApp.

The fourth and final usability test will be your actual software prototype. In this phase, you are testing usage and adoption.

Just as you compiled interview data to spot patterns of what people need, you'll also compile feedback from your usability tests at each stage as your prototypes become more and more refined. Spot the consistent comments about what is confusing or could be improved, and be sure to understand why. The feedback that these initial customers provide is invaluable and should be incorporated to improve your product's design.

Exercise 7.5: Create an interactive prototype of your product

Objective: Create an interactive prototype for more usability testing.

Directions:

1. Select a wireframing tool.[40]

2. Wireframe storyboards from Exercise 7.3 or using the wireframes and feedback from your paper prototype.

3. When you're creating wireframes, you'll want to make sure that the design elements are consistent. Buttons, links, and other page elements should look the same across the product.

4. Be sure to simulate interactions customers will have with the elements.

5. Don't get too hung up on the exact interface (e.g., horizontal tabs versus vertical tabs). Focus more on the interactions and how data will flow between screens.

   You can use this clickable prototype to conduct more usability tests, and then use it as a basis for high-fidelity mockups and an actual software prototype.

Review

Design is a great way of differentiating your product. However, there are a lot of layers when it comes to designing your product. First, revisit the personas and behavioral descriptions you created in Chapter 6, and focus on the verbs that are common to the personas—or just focus on building for one persona.

Next, understand the tasks that go into the verbs and break those tasks down into user stories with clear goals. The user stories will support the creation of features.

Before you dive into building features, you'll want to validate your design. You can validate it with a paper prototype by drawing workflows, performing a usability test on customers, and collecting feedback. With more and more learnings, you can create increasingly refined prototypes and conduct more usability tests.

What you've validated in this chapter

If you completed the exercises in this chapter then you should have validated the following:

- The design of your competitor's product doesn't meet the needs of your ideal customer segment.

- A customer's beliefs lead to behaviors and those behaviors manifest into tasks.

- Which tasks are important to customers (not every task is worth emulating in software, and customers indicate a natural priority through their beliefs and desires).

- The design of the workflows using a paper prototype and performing usability tests on customers.

Chapter 8

What to Put in a Prototype

Here's one of the most common stories I hear from people who reach out to me: *"I'm really stuck, I'm tired, and I'm about to burn out. I've rebuilt this product 6 times and we've had 10K people download it (or 10M people sign up), but we just cannot monetize. I don't know what to do or what to build to get people to pay for our product."*

So then I ask them 2 very basic questions: *"What is your value proposition? And, what problem are you trying to solve?"*

Their response is a head scratch, followed by, *"What do you mean, we built this thing."* And they point to the product.

I dig in a little deeper: *"Well, what problem does it solve?"*

They're just not sure. It's composed of a lot of features.

So then I move on and ask them, *"Who are your customers?"*

And they respond with something generic like, *"Uhh, women..."*

That's when I have to tell them, *"Stop building! Don't build anything more."*

Of course, they are baffled. *"You're an engineer, why are you telling us not to build anything?"*

"Your problem is not that you don't know how to build a product or that you don't know how to get people to try it out. The problem is that you don't know how to convey the value of your product to people. So you don't have an engineering problem, which is why I don't want you to build anything more. I want you to think about your value proposition."

You might be in a similar situation if you've already built your product: you don't know how to monetize your customers. Or, you might just be stuck trying to attract them.

Let's take a step back and identify the true value you can provide to your customers. This will help you decide what to put in a prototype and help you run experiments to learn whether your product idea meets customer needs.

Section 1

What's your value proposition?

Before building anything, it's important to understand who the early adopter of your product is and what your product's value proposition is. A value proposition is a certain experience or benefit that a customer can expect to receive from your product or service in exchange for money.

Notice that this definition does not include, *"My product has XYZ feature."*

Here are a couple examples of value propositions from BizeeBee:

1. *Stop losing money on expired memberships!* (Revenue is the value proposition here.)

2. *Use a simple solution to avoid losing money on expired memberships.* (Revenue and simplicity are the value propositions.)

Here are a couple from Mint:

1. *Navigate the credit card jungle with our free web-based money intelligence software.*

2. *Stop losing money on unknown fees. Put money back in your pocket with our free web-based money intelligence software.*

Notice that in both of these examples, we're not talking about how we're going to do this (i.e., features). We're just focused on the value (i.e., benefits customers will experience).

Unfortunately, if you prioritize building over validating an idea, the result may have little to no traction. This can be demotivating for most and eventually lead to burnout.

If you've been following along with the exercises in this book, by now you've conducted a number of customer interviews, followed up by doing usability tests with paper prototypes, and created interactive wireframes. Through each stage, you should have received a lot of feedback. The feedback should give you a pretty good sense of what the acute needs of early adopters are. You'll now need to translate those into value propositions.

Exercise 8.1: List your product's value propositions.

Objective: To test out value propositions and see which ones people will sign up for.

Directions:

1. Similar to the list I've created above for BizeeBee and Mint, come up with some value propositions you are testing. Remember, it should only include benefits, not features!

2. Talk about the benefits with your customers and ask them if those are the key benefits they are looking for in your product.

It's important that you nail down the copy for your value propositions, because you'll be reusing them in Chapter 10. If you're not sure what the best copy is, then keep all your variations, and you can test them out later.

You might be ready and eager to build a prototype or, as we call it in the biz, an **MVP (minimum viable product)**.

Given that a startup is dealing with a lot of uncertainty and has limited resources, I advise startup founders to start with a "concierge MVP."

Section 2

Start with a concierge MVP

A concierge MVP is an experience, not a product. Essentially, you're initially offering a service. You service the customer, keep track of all the steps, and once you have a critical mass of customers you can switch to automating the service through a software product.

You can also do a hybrid: offer a slimmed-down software product as a solution and manually perform the services for the remainder of what you are offering to customers.

Instead of jumping into building a product, you take the time to create a hypothesis of who your early adopters might be. Next, you create a hypothesis of what value proposition would appeal to the early adopters. Once both the hypotheses are set, you then proceed to create an experience that will help you test both of these hypotheses. Even if your ultimate goal is to create a technology or a physical product, you should start by crafting an experience. As you approach early adopters and receive feedback, you can focus your efforts on what actually needs to be built.

For example, when I was getting started with BizeeBee, before building the CRM solution, I created a 1-page ad listing the product's benefits—basically a landing page (I'll explain how to do that in the chapter on scrappy marketing strategies). Those who were interested in trying out the product could enter their email addresses, and I'd notify them when we launched.

Note that it doesn't matter what type of software product you are creating. The purpose of the concierge MVP is to give people a taste of the value prop and collect feedback from them so that you can go on to create an actual product.

There are 2 other benefits to starting with a concierge MVP:

1. You establish a very close connection with your early adopters, making it easier for them to open up to you and provide feedback.

2. You'll reduce your iteration cycle. You can quickly change your messaging to reflect a different value proposition or attract a different type of early adopter if you find that what you initially put out isn't attracting anyone.

It's important for both technical and non-technical founders to start with a concierge MVP.

When I say this, I usually hear groans from both technical and non-technical founders. They push back, telling me that customers want to see and play with a product before they can determine its value.

Here is where the misunderstanding begins. Too often, we think a product's value comes from features, when really, customers value a product for its benefits.

It doesn't matter what "product" you sell to early adopters. They are interested in experiencing the benefits you spoke about, which you can give them using a concierge MVP.

Examples of companies that began as concierge MVPs

Now, you might still be skeptical. So I'm going to showcase a few successful companies that began as concierge MVPs. You might even be shocked to know that one of these has become a billion-dollar company!

 Case Study

Zappos began with a hybrid MVP model

The founder of Zappos, Nick, loved shoes, and had a hypothesis that other people probably loved shoes just as much as he did. He also hypothesized that people might be open to buying shoes online. But he wasn't 100% sure. So the first thing he did was walk into a shoe store in San Francisco. He asked the shoe store owner about current inventory. Then he struck up a deal: every time someone bought a pair of shoes on his website, he'd come over and purchase the shoes from the store owner. The store owner agreed to the deal. Nick went home and set up a pretty simple site listing the inventory that was in the store.

Guess what happened next? Nick sold his first pair of shoes, then his second, and so on.

By offering a manual service through a concierge MVP, Nick validated his theory that people will buy shoes online. The value proposition was clear to early adopters: it was convenient to search through an inventory of shoes and purchase online.

Only after Nick had validated his business model through his concierge MVP did he approach Tony Hsieh for funds.

 ## Case Study

AirBnB started out by offering a simple service

Many people have witnessed the rise of AirBnB and experienced how easy it is to find and book a rental online. However, before AirBnB became what it is today, it started off as a simple side project for the 3 founders, and is probably one of the most classic examples of a concierge MVP.

Days before the Democratic National Convention, the 3 founders knew that people wouldn't be able to find a place to stay. So they piled up air beds (hence AirBnB) into their small apartment and put up a simple ad about renting an air bed. Guess what? People actually rented an air bed!

The value proposition was clear: people who wanted to go to this highly sold-out event couldn't find a place to stay in traditional places such as hotels and B&Bs. So the 3 AirBnB founders were able to offer them a place, and their early adopters were willing to pay and sleep on air beds.

In both of these cases, Zappos and AirBnB eventually did a lot to scale their businesses and become million- and billion-dollar revenue generators. But by starting with concierge MVPs, they were able to test out their first hypotheses without making huge investments in terms of time and resources to build a full product. They were able to prove that people would buy the experience.

OK, hopefully by this point you're starting to see the value in creating a concierge MVP. But you're probably wondering how to begin. In the next section, I will walk you through how to get started!

Section 4

What should I put in an MVP?

You can either have a concierge MVP that is 100% experiential or you can build some of it out with software. If you choose to build, then you'll want to review sentiments from interviews and usability tests and create two lists of features: Must-Haves vs. Nice-to-Haves. Below is an example using my lists from BizeeBee.

Must-Haves

- Record student information, such as name and contact info.

- Track memberships to see who is in the clear and who is expired or "in the red."

- Track how many students come to each class.

- Track how much money the business has made month-over-month.

- Collect money more easily than harassing students at the end of each class to keep the business alive!

Nice-to-Haves

- A way to send out reminders to pull students back if they haven't visited the business in a while.

- A schedule where people can book themselves into a class.

- Keep data on a need-to-know basis with other staff members.

Remember, the Must-Haves should reflect the value propositions you're testing. Let's assume that these Must-Haves will go into our MVP, and we'll build the Nice-to-Haves eventually.

In the next chapter, I'll explain how you are going to share this with potential teammates.

Next, you want to make sure that you are differentiating your MVP. We're back to positioning again!

To differentiate, think beyond the product:

- What will the first-time experience be for customers?

- How will you onboard them?

- What level of customer service would you like to provide?

- Are you displacing a competitor or providing an add-on solution?

Exercise 8.2: Come up with a list of Must-Haves.

Objective: Identify the features you need to include in your prototype based on the interview data and have make sure they tie into the value propositions you listed in Exercise 8.1.

Directions:

1. Go back to the tasks you created in Chapter 7 Exercise 7.2, comb through interview data to find the common pain points that customers were experiencing, then create your list of Must-Haves.

2. List the Must-Haves under the value propositions. If one doesn't fit, then you'll need to either skip the Must-Have or modify the value proposition (remember, it still needs to reflect the benefit of the feature, not the feature itself).

   If your list is very long, you'll need to whittle it down further based on what is feasible in your launch timeframe.

Finally, you might want to review the list with customers to make sure that these are indeed the features that are most important to them and that they're aligned with the value propositions.

Exercise 8.3: Refine your storyboards.

Objective: Marry the storyboards with the Must-Have features and make sure they reflect the value proposition(s) you are testing in your MVP.

Directions:

1. Remember those storyboards you created in Chapter 7 Exercise 7.3? I want you to pull them out. If you didn't create storyboards for your Must-Haves, then create them now.

2. Remember the ideal customer you created in Chapter 6 Exercise 6.2? It's time to get into character again. Pretend you are that customer and walk through the storyboards.

3. Does the experience you went through in the storyboards tie back to the value proposition you're testing? If you're not sure, run the storyboards by a customer.

4. Once your storyboard experience, Must-Haves list, and value propositions are all aligned, you are good to go. But until then, you'll want to take the time to refine the experience.

I know this might seem like a lot of steps and work, but remember, the point is to validate your idea as much as possible before we jump into building so that we don't waste time and resources building a product people don't want!

Review

Just a quick recap. You're creating an MVP to test two things: the value proposition and the early adopter segment.

I recommend starting with a concierge MVP even before you build out a software prototype. A concierge MVP is an experience, not a product. Based on the experience, you can get a sense of what resonates with early adopters, and once they've validated the experience you can move on to investing in building a software prototype.

We'll cover how to go about recruiting a team and building out the software prototype in the next chapter!

What you've validated in this chapter

If you completed the exercises in this chapter then you should have validated the following:

- Your product's value proposition is appealing to customers and will convince them to use your product without having to list specific features.
- Early adopters might be open to a concierge MVP, in which case you may not need to build a prototype initially.
- Your product prototype's Must-Haves are aligned with your value proposition.

Interview with Ben Congleton, CEO and Co-founder of Olark

Olark[41] is a live chat software service that helps businesses boost sales, resolve issues, and understand their customers.

Olark was founded in 2009 by Ben Congleton, Matt Pizzimenti, Roland Osborne and Zach Steindler. Initially funded by seed accelerator Y Combinator, Olark has gone on to profitable success by providing a compelling product and amazing service.

Olark is headquartered in the arboreal oasis of South Park, San Francisco. It also has an office in Ann Arbor, MI, their "hometown," as well as employees across the US, Canada, Brazil, and the U.K.

As you read my interview with Ben, you'll learn how he got into programming at a young age, developed his first business in the early days of the Internet, and what eventually led him to start Olark.

Poornima: "Hi Ben! I've known you for many years now, but I don't know how you got into programming. Let's start there."

Ben: "My freshman year of high school I started by just modifying scripts, and noticed that my cousin Roland was building cooler things than me. So I picked up a copy of *Teach Yourself Perl in 21 days.*"

Poornima: "Yeah, I think I had a copy of that too! How did that lead you into starting your first business?"

Ben: "I was tired of wasting time on the Internet playing video games. So, I started an IT consulting company programming PHP and installing code on websites. Then, in 1998 I started a web hosting company called Nethernet, which eventually became Netherweb, with my cousin Roland."

Poornima: "Since you were in high school, how did you have any money to start a business?"

Ben: "We got a $100 investment from Roland's dad to buy nethernet.com. I learned to bootstrap early on, and by my senior year of high school we were making $170K in revenue."

Poornima: "How did you get over customers' perceptions when they knew you were just a kid?"

Ben: "We were just online, so no one knew who we really were."

Poornima: "Haha. That's awesome! So then how did you attract customers?"

Ben: "At the time, there were sites like Yelp for hosting companies. I focused on providing awesome support and got good referrals. There was also a ranking engine and we figured out how to get to the top of it by offering a low-price plan. Then we wrote a free software program that got showcased in PC Magazine."

Poornima: "Wow, so you had some really scalable tactics. OK, so let's switch gears. You were making $170K your senior year, so why did you decide to go to college? Why not just build the business?"

Ben: "I wanted to have a real life, and the business helped pay for college. It was a great source of passive income, and we worked on it for a few days a week."

Poornima: "And how did your business grow when you were in college?"

Ben: "It didn't. I hired other people to do support, and we eventually lost touch with our customers. It was slowly dying because we weren't working and competition got crazy. There were a lot of well-funded companies, and hosting was starting to become a commodity."

Poornima: "OK, so what did you do next?"

Ben: "I graduated with degrees in Computer Science and Business from Virginia Tech. An advisor convinced me to get a Masters in Computer Science. I started to think about going the academic route. So I applied for a PhD at the University of Michigan's HCI [human computer interaction] program. I was still running the business on the side. Roland and Kevin, a friend of mine, were working on it full time, and it became a consulting firm. Then in 2006, when I was at University of Michigan, I went to a seminar about how the Internet affords disintermediation. Businesses can talk directly to consumers through phone or email. I thought about chat, because that's what our generation grew up with. We used AIM or ICQ."

Poornima: "Yeah, I used AIM a lot in high school. So how did that seminar inspire you?"

Ben: "I figured there was an opportunity to provide the same functionality as peer-to-peer communication. Businesses could talk directly to customers through chat."

Poornima: "So what happened to the consulting business?"

Ben: "I was sick of consulting, but we used it to fund product development. In 2007, Kevin and I built the first version of Olark—back then we called it Habla. It was a free product and businesses could use it to talk to customers. We integrated with existing IM clients."

Poornima: "That is a great bootstrapping strategy, and one that I recommend too! So what was the feedback on the prototype?"

Ben: "It was really buggy, because it was a fast prototype. I was too busy adding support for AIM, ICQ, and MSN. We needed someone to lead engineering. Roland was really focused on design, and I wanted to focus on product and the business."

Poornima: "How did you go about recruiting?"

Ben: "We went through a number of co-founders. It was really hard getting people to commit. There were like, '*yeah, we'll join once X happens.*' They didn't like being remote or had other personal commitments like mortgages. Then in the fall of 2008, we applied to YC [Y Combinator]."

Poornima: "That must have been pretty exciting."

Ben: "Yeah, but the market was pretty bad, so they deferred us for 6 months. We then applied to TechStars and found another co-founder, Matt. Matt was the perfect person; he was a really good engineer, and he went all-in very quickly."

Poornima: "Where did you meet Matt?"

Ben: "At a PhD networking event."

Poornima: "Did you end up going to YC or TechStars?"

Ben: "We interviewed, got into YC, and then moved the team to Mountain View."

Poornima: "What was YC like?'

Ben: "We received $25K from YC and focused on launching the paid version of the product. We were making $25 per day in 2009."

Poornima: "YC demo days are pretty happening. What was yours like? And were you able to raise capital?"

Ben: "We were not the hottest company. It was probably WePay or MixPanel. We tried to raise, like, $400K, but it seemed like it would take a long time. So, we ended up raising $60K from friends and family."

Poornima: "So your focus became profitability?"

Ben: "Yeah. We raised prices and doubled down on our conversion funnel [getting customers to convert from free to paid]."

Poornima: "How did you do that?"

Ben: "We just focused on making it super easy to integrate Olark on your site. By the end of 2009, we became 'Ramen profitable,' and were making $100/day."

Poornima: "What did you do to grow?"

Ben: "We gave it [our service] to other startups in YC, then partnered with the Small Business Web and e-commerce shopping carts like Shopify. We really just focused on making our product work, and that has led to lots of traffic."

Poornima: "Yeah, I like how Olark has baked-in marketing. I remember that when we met back in 2010, you had a singular vision: live chat. Has that changed at all?"

Ben: "We say no to all ideas that aren't focused on helping businesses talk to their customers."

Poornima: "It's great to have focus. Well, it's been 7 years since you started—have you ever had a moment when things got too hard or you wanted to quit?"

Ben: "We've always been focused on building a good team internally and attracting the right customers. That has kept me engaged."

Poornima: "That is great to hear, thank you Ben!"

Just to recap, here's what we learned from Ben Congleton:

1. **You can start a business at any age.** Ben began his first business while he was still in high school and had just learned how to program.

2. **You can bootstrap your business to profitability.** While other companies from YC went on to raise significant amounts of capital, Ben and his team decided to focus on generating recurring revenue and getting to Ramen profitability.

3. **Finding co-founders takes a few tries.** It took Ben and Roland a while to assemble the right team, but they kept at it.

4. **Focus on building a product that is easy to use for your customers.** Ben and his team were able to go from $25/day to $100/day by making it easy to integrate Olark into websites.

Chapter 9

How to Manage Product Development and Attract Top Technical Talent

Do you remember how you felt on the first day of your first real job? If you're like me, then you were probably stoked! I could hardly sleep the night before. I was eager to learn the system and start writing code.

But much to my chagrin, my manager spent the whole day introducing me to people on the team. As lunchtime rolled around, he got everyone together and we headed out the door.

Now, don't get me wrong—I love to eat and was thrilled to have a team lunch on the first day. We went to this awesome Singaporean restaurant, and I had the lamb shank. But as I chowed down on the shank, what I really wanted to be doing was digging into the code base and building!

At lunch, one of my colleagues leaned over and said, *"This is the honeymoon period, enjoy it! The boss doesn't expect you to produce anything for the first 3-6 months."*

What?!

That is not what I had signed up for.

It turns out that he didn't expect me to produce anything because there wasn't a clear roadmap for the product or what I'd be doing.

I understood that being the lowest on the food chain meant that I'd be doing whatever work people assigned to me, but I still wanted to know what was coming along.

A few years later as I was getting the boot from my first job, I realized why the team and I never quite clicked. I needed to be under a leader who had a vision. I needed to know where we were headed and what we were going to do next, even if we didn't necessarily do it immediately, so that I could plan and build accordingly.

If you build products without a plan, are you shooting from the hip or shooting yourself in the foot?

Too often, I come across people who sway from one extreme to the other. They are the mavericks who scoff when they hear the word "plan," preferring to shoot from the hip. Eventually, shooting from the hip gets tiring, both for the maverick and their team.

Engineers understand the process of building something quick and dirty, then refining it over time. But plans that keep changing under a maverick leader irk them. They feel like they're building for a moving target. Eventually they lose motivation (learn more about the psychology behind this at the Femgineer blog: "How to Keep Your Startup Engineer Sane"[42]). To stay motivated, engineers need to understand the product's direction and vision. It's OK to have changes, but constant changes for days or weeks means that there is no vision.

On the flip side, I've seen other leaders who get so hell-bent on following a plan to the T that they make the organization rigid. They take an all-or-nothing attitude if deadlines aren't met. This also can cause teams to burn out!

Of course, when you're building something new, you can expect unforeseen circumstances to arise.

To deal with them, you need to have a rough outline of product milestones.

Section 1

Product roadmap

The plan I'm encouraging you to produce is actually an outline called a product roadmap. It will provide direction for where you are headed. There are a number of ways to produce a product roadmap. Pick whichever one you feel fits your style, but do make one!

Here's an example of the roadmap we had in the second and third year of BizeeBee.

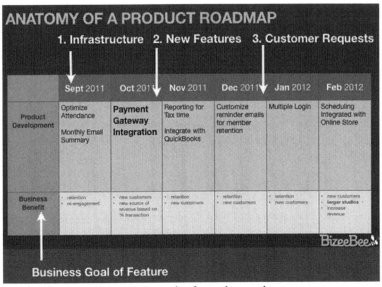

Figure 9.1 Example of a product roadmap.

Notice a few things: first, we have listed all the high-level features that we are going to build. Next, we classify them as either infrastructure projects, new features, or customer requests. The reason we classify them is to give everyone on the team a high-level understanding of all the things that need to be built. It also shows that it's not easy to just build one thing; there are layers they need to think about.

At the bottom, you'll notice that I state the "Business Benefit." The **business benefit** is basically a business metric, and I'll explain analytics and **metrics** in-depth in Chapter 12. For now, know that a metric is how you measure business performance (for example, the percentage of free to paying customers is a business metric known as **conversion rate**).

The primary reason you include business metrics in your product roadmap is to make sure that what you are building is aligned with your high-level business goals.

Too often, I see business goals at odds with product milestones in organizations. This is caused by a lack of transparency and communication, as well as too many goals or unclear ones. The results are missed deadlines and employees who are burnt out.

I've limited this particular roadmap to the work of a product team. However, you can also have additional rows for sales, marketing, and customer support projects along with their business unit metrics. Once again, there should be alignment. For example, if the product team is putting out a new feature, then sales and marketing should probably come up with a project to make sure that prospective customers and existing customers know about it through a campaign.

The product roadmap is not set in stone. It is meant to be a high-level representation of what you'd like to build, but what gets built depends on resources—talent, money, and time—and their availability can affect your roadmap.

In the roadmap above for BizeeBee, you'll notice that we thought Payment Gateway Integration was going to take 1 month. It actually ended up taking 8 months to build! We were OK with that, given our team size. The reason it took us longer than a month was that we needed to research the companies that offer payment APIs, sift through them, and then decide on a partner we could trust. Since this was one of our highest priorities, everything else slated for production in November 2011 and onward was placed on the back burner.

Depending on the stage you're at, that product roadmap can be 3 to 6 weeks out or 3 to 6 months out. In the beginning, start with weeks. The rough roadmap should highlight the things you need to do each week or month, allowing you to track major milestones. If something comes up that demands resources, then it needs to be reviewed next to the original outline so you can understand what its priority is.

If you don't have an engineer to create a plan for, I know what you're thinking. *"This is a side project ... Why do I need to be concerned about a team? Right now, it's just me!"*

Yes, it's true. I did say you're starting this off as a side project. However, at some point you'll realize you cannot do it all. You will need to get some help. I'll dig into how to recruit teammates in an upcoming section, but for now, realize that the roadmap will help you and others understand where you are headed.

Two final things I'll say about having a roadmap. The first is that once you've got it set up, you also know what you can do if things go well. I call these **accelerators**. Let's say, for example, you make more money than you intended, receive funding, or finish a project ahead of schedule. Now you can accelerate the development of what is next on the roadmap.

The second is that when you revisit a roadmap later, know that it may be outdated, especially if your business goals have changed. So before proceeding, you'll need to revise it.

Exercise 9.1: Create a 4-week product roadmap with high-level features you want to build.

Objective: Get comfortable creating a product roadmap, sharing it with teammates, and receiving feedback.

Don't worry about setting business metrics for now; you'll be adding those in a future lesson.

Directions:

1. List out the 4 weeks.

2. Remember that list of Must-Haves from Chapter 8 Exercise 8.2? Use those, and list out a Must-Have feature you want to build for each week. For now, I recommend one feature per week.

3. Many of the Must-Haves are going to be new features and customer requests, so be sure to take stock of infrastructure that you need to build in order to support those Must-Haves.

4. Categorize all the features listed into the following buckets: infrastructure, new features, customer requests, bugs, etc.

5. Make sure you've taken into account dependencies and listed them in chronological order.

6. Do you expect anything to accelerate development of those features, like money or additional help? If so, make a note of that.

7. Share this roadmap with your teammates and solicit feedback.

Section 2

Break features down into user stories

In Chapter 7 Exercise 7.2, I had you come up with user stories. We're going to reuse those and break them down further! I know what you're thinking: *"This feels like a lot of process just to get set up. Can't we start building already and then get feedback from customers?"*

I agree that it feels lame, and I know you're eager to build. So just bear with me while I share a simple example to explain why it's important to create user stories for all your features.

Have you ever picked out a recipe and thought, *"Oh, it's just mac and cheese, how hard could it be? How long could it possibly take? 15 minutes, tops!"* So you yell to your significant other, *"Don't worry hun, I gotz this!"*

You read over the recipe to discover it's not Easy Mac & Cheese from a box, it's fancy mac and cheese ... might as well call it mac et fromage. You need special pasta that takes 30 minutes to cook instead of 3 minutes, you need 4 kinds of cheese, and you'll need to sauté onions (and not just any type of onion, but fancy ones, like shallots). Then, you have to bake the whole thing for another 30-45 minutes and let it cool before you can dig in!

Pretty soon, your sig-o in the other room has passed out from hunger. (Side note: in this particular example, I'm the sig-o that passes out. But I'm also a foodie and hate stuff from a box. I love my boyfriend's mac et fromage and pretty much all French food, so it's usually worth the wait!)

Well, in software, we call this scope creep. You originally have an estimate in your head, but then you start to discover that the project is way more complex that you had originally expected. So instead of taking the estimated time, it takes 2-3 times or even 10 times as long!

One of the main reasons people miss deadlines is because they fail to factor in complexities, such as how difficult is it to build what you want to build, and whether you or your team needs time to learn how to build it.

To prevent this from happening as you are building your product, you want to take the time to break down a feature into user stories and observe how complex they are.

Sometimes people call very large features an **epic**. This helps distinguish the simple and easy-to-create features from the ones that are layered or rely on others. It also connotes the complexity and time required to build them.

It might not seem like a big deal now, but distinguishing between stories, features, and epics will make conversations go smoother. It sets the context of the conversations and signals to technical folks that you are acknowledging that each feature is different, and that some are harder or take longer to build than others.

Let's recall the formula for a user story:

persona + task + goal

Let me break it down further:

who is performing the task + what the task is + the end goal for performing the task

Here's a simple example feature: a user login. The business goal for creating a user login is to give users a private account with which they can access their data.

We'll call the high-level feature (epic) a "user login flow."

Next, we'll break down all the steps that a user needs to do in order to create a user login.

1. *As a user, I need a login in order to access my own account.* (High-level feature)

2. *As a user, I need to enter a valid email address and password in order to create a login.* (First story)

But this story isn't actually basic. It brings up questions like *"what is a valid email address and password?"*

Whenever you're creating stories and people bring up clarification questions, that's a good thing; it helps identify the scope of the story. If you tell people to hush their concerns and say things like, "Eh, it doesn't matter," you are setting yourself up for scope creep.

Exercise 9.2: Break a feature down into user stories.

Objective: Get comfortable breaking down a feature into user stories.

Directions:

1. Pick one feature you listed in the product roadmap.

2. Break it down into as many stories as you can think of using the formula:

   who is performing the task + what the task is + the end goal for performing the task

3. Identify and make a note of dependencies among stories.

Section 3

Nobody likes a creep.

Scope creep is a byproduct of complexity. It happens when you don't anticipate every scenario, miscalculate how long it will take to build something, or don't include the time it takes to learn how to build it.

It's OK if it happens—it's only natural. However, when scope creep does happen, you have to stop and do three things:

1. Write down the issue.

2. Break it down into simple user stories.

3. Prioritize it against what people are already working on, because it might not be a big deal and can wait.

Let's go back to our example above. We'll want to add the following stories to avoid scope creep as much as possible:

1. *As a user, in order to create a login, I need to enter a valid email address, which means that it contains alphanumeric characters and a dot followed by a valid ending (net, com, co, org, etc.).*

2. *As a user, I should receive a verification email to ensure that I didn't fat-finger my email address.*

OK, by now you get the idea. You want to dig in and create as many stories as possible.

Once that's done, you'll note priorities and dependencies because you cannot ship an incomplete feature.

I remember back when we first shipped BizeeBee. We completely forgot to write code to recover a password. We only realized it right after we shipped, and a customer complained that they had forgotten their password. We immediately built it out and shipped it.

Hopefully the *mac et fromage* has burned into your mind the idea that estimating is difficult for humans. However, I know you'll start to build and try to create estimates for stories, or demand them from others.

It's really OK if you do—I'm just warning you to set your expectations.

Figure 9.2

As you identify, organize, and prioritize features to build, I highly recommend using a tool like **Pivotal Tracker** (image above).[43] In Tracker you'll have a few buckets, such as a "done" bucket for what has been shipped, and "backlog," which is a list of stories that have been prioritized. The top of the queue should be what someone is currently working on, and preferably that's just one story. As people complete stories they are to pick off what's at the top of the backlog to work on. These keep teams humming along. Next, there is "icebox," a list of all uncompleted stories that haven't been prioritized. Finally, there's a "releases" bucket, in case you have multiple releases.

In Tracker, you assign each story a point value from 2 to 8, 8 being the most complex or time consuming (note: sometimes the most time-consuming tasks aren't necessarily complex). As each person is handed a story, they are to provide estimates for how long they think it will take to complete.

Next, you set a release marker and drag stories over to it so you know which stories are going into each release. You can set a deadline for the release or leave it as-is.

As you and your team completes stories, Tracker monitors your progress and records the point values for the completed stories. It will notify you once you've finished everything, and if you had a release date set, you'll see whether you're on or off target. You might decide to still ship if there are no dependencies, or hold off.

Tracker will tell you how accurate your estimate was over multiple release cycles. If you and your team are pretty accurate, you'll have what's known as a high velocity score. If you're way off, Tracker will give you a high *volatility* score, which basically describes how far off you are. You will, of course, have to figure out why you were off yourself.

I know this was quite a meaty lesson, but I want to make sure you have a product development process in place. It doesn't have to be perfect or rigid, but it should hold you and your teammates accountable and let you know where you're headed!

Exercise 9.3: Track user stories.

Objectives: Get in the habit of tracking user stories to stay up-to-date with your product-building progress.

Directions:

1.   Pick a tool for tracking like Pivotal Tracker.

2. List out all the features (epics) you are building.

3. List out all the user stories that coincide with those features. Make sure you've broken them down to as small a unit as possible.

4. Create a priority order of the user stories. If you have teammates, you'll want to create the prioritized list with them.

5. Create a release marker for when you expect a particular feature to be done. I highly recommend starting with just one feature that is independent (i.e., can be released without having to build other features).

6. As you and your teammates complete stories, mark them as done.

7. If you experience scope creep, you'll want to include those user stories. You'll also want to revisit the priority, chronological ordering of the stories, and any dependencies between stories.

8. Keep track of how long it takes you to complete the stories, how much scope creep added to your time frame, and how close or far off you were at estimating releasing the feature.

Keep in mind that this process will take some time to get used to, and you might need to refine it based on your team's needs. However, it will help you make progress and ship code to customers!

Section 4

Who's going to build this product?

It might feel like there is a dearth of technical talent available, but the reality is that there's a dearth of *high-quality* technical talent. In this section and in the next, I'm going to suggest some approaches for how you can go about building your initial prototype and how you can go about recruiting technical talent.

The first thing I want you to realize is that recruiting is a sales process. This means it's just like trying to sell your product to customers; you are trying to sell the benefits of working for you and with you to potential employees or teammates.

Marc Benioff, the co-founder and CEO of Salesforce says, *"The secret to successful hiring is this: look for people who want to change the world."*

What Benioff is getting at is that you need to sell people on the vision for your product. A vision isn't a high-level overview of what your product does and whom it's for. Rather, it describes the positive impact you want to make on people's lives. In other words: *why* you do what you do.

Section 5

The right time to recruit

There is a right time to recruit. That time is when you have decent sense of what needs to be built. This doesn't mean that you have to know that it is THE right thing to build. It just means that you are committed to building something. If you aren't committed, then your teammates won't be either!

This is not the stage where you want to hire a recruiter. Instead, I recommend you meet technical talent at conferences and meetups. If you don't have any near you, then use online channels like Dribbble, Twitter, Stackoverflow, Reddit, and Github. Technical folks are even more receptive to these channels than LinkedIn, because it's where they hang out!

The next step is to gauge the candidate's experience level and interest. This is the step that a lot of non-technical folks worry about. They think they have no way of knowing whether someone is a good engineer—or, if they're hiring a designer, whether the candidate actually did the design work in their portfolio. Some folks even resort to learning to code just to help them judge the level of a candidate's technical talent.

Well, let me ask you this: do you know how to build a home? Unless you're an architect, most likely not. So, what do people do when they decide to build a home?

In the US, most people hire a contractor, but before they hire the contractor they probably go through steps like these:

- Comb through a list of contractors.
- Pare it down to the ones they can afford and are of the quality they are looking for.
- Ask for reference customers.
- Read reviews.

What they don't do is ask them questions like, *"How do you lay down foundation?" "What kind of bricks do you prefer to use?"*

No, they leave all that to the contractor. The same principles apply here. If you are non-technical, focus on figuring out if the candidate is credible and competent. There are ways to do that without you learning how to code.

If you're still concerned, then give them a mini-project. Some people hate this because they feel like they have to do free work. So what I usually do is pay people a small amount and keep the project to about a week. This lets me answer the following questions:

1. Can they deliver something on time?
2. Do I enjoy working with them?
3. What is the quality of the finished project?

If you're on the fence about which candidate to choose, give your top 3 candidates a mini-project.

What's most important is that you have a firm understanding of your needs and communicate them clearly! Whatever the requirements for a project are, including budget and deadlines, share them with people instead of keeping the candidate guessing. If they can meet the requirements, they'll let you know. If they can't, then you can move on and find a better fit.

Section 6

Working for sweat equity

Sweat equity is when you just pay people in equity—that's it. Unfortunately, too many technical folks have been taken advantage of in deals like this, so many are reluctant to only take equity in a company.

My personal bias is to pay people something, even if it's just a little bit, just to make it clear that I value their efforts but I have limited means. Then, I leave it up to them to decide whether it's enough. If it's not, then I'll keep looking, and if it is enough for now, great!

If I'm bringing someone on as a co-founder, then I may not pay them, because they are getting a really big equity stake. But for everyone else, I think it's important that people feel like they are being compensated fairly.

Section 7

In-house, remote, or outsourced?

I've had teams that are in-house, remote, and outsourced. In-house is great if you have the capital and really care about seeing everyone face-to-face each day. However, I've also built a remote team over the years and have outsourced a lot of projects to contractors. The common element to making each of these succeed is communication.

People think that it's hard to communicate when you're miles apart or in a different time zone. However, I know teams who sit next to each other every day and don't exchange a single word!

Ultimately, you need to build the team that is going to support your efforts and long-term vision. If you want to have an in-house team, great. You'll need to figure out office space, rent, and make sure everyone is cool with commuting in.

If you want to set up a remote team, then figure out how you're going to communicate daily using email, chat, and video conferencing. I'd still encourage you to get some live face-to-face time with your teammates. I love doing team retreats annually or biannually and know other teams who do the same.

If you decide to go the route of outsourcing, then you need to communicate what needs to be done clearly and make sure you have agreed to check-in times.

I love to outsource projects that have no dependencies on the rest of my team and aren't tied to product deadlines. For example, a few years ago I hired a designer in Sri Lanka to build BizeeBee's landing site. Since this wasn't on the same path as the product, I gave him all the requirements and put my marketing person in charge of interfacing with him. The rest of the team continued to build the product and weren't fazed by this other project that was going on behind the scenes.

Section 8

Build versus buy

Whichever path you choose—hiring someone or building the product yourself—there will come a time when you will be faced with a decision to build a feature yourself or buy an existing solution.

For example, remember the Payment Gateway Integration feature I listed in the BizeeBee product roadmap in Section 1? We could have built the whole thing in-house, except that it would have cost us $150K+ and taken at least 2 years. Not to mention that we didn't have expertise in payments. Instead of building, we decided to go with a vendor who was an expert at the system. Then, I had my engineers integrate the vendors' solution into our product.

Our decision came down to cost of ownership, which we broke into 2 parts: the cost to build it and the cost to maintain it. Totaling the two up, we realized it was significantly cheaper to buy the solution from a vendor.

We came to the same conclusion when our customers asked us for email. Instead of building an email solution, we simply integrated our product with an existing email provider, MadMimi.

Just like it's important to interview candidates you want to hire, the same is true if you decide to buy a solution. You must take the time to research vendors, understand how long it's going to take to integrate their products into yours, and reach out to customers to get the real backstory with respect to the quality of their product and customer service. You also want to ask some probing questions about how long they have been in business and how many customers they have, because the last thing you want is to do business with someone who is brand new, doesn't know what they're doing, or is in danger of going under!

Two final caveats. The first is that if you decide to go down the path of partnering with a vendor, know that the relationship doesn't need to be exclusive. You should be free to choose other vendors. The second is that there may come a time where the relationship gets strained; you might outgrow them or their level of service doesn't meet your needs.

If this happens, you'll once again need to reevaluate whether you want to build or buy. If you have grown by then, it might make sense to build. If it still doesn't make sense from a cost-of-ownership perspective, then you might want to look for another vendor.

Section 9

Keeping teams happy and productive

It's not enough to just recruit people to your team. You also need to think about how you'll communicate, check in with each other, and resolve conflicts. Too often, people wait until a situation escalates (e.g., a teammate is really unhappy, quits, or threatens to quit).

I'm going to take a page from one of my favorite books: The 5 Dysfunctions of a Team.

Figure 9.3

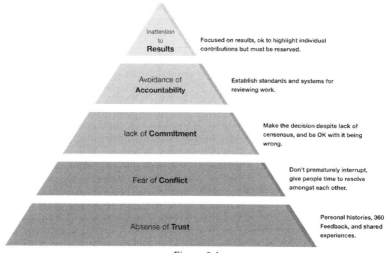

Figure 9.4

Dealing with departures

No matter how amazing a leader or visionary you are, people will still leave, and that's OK! They leave because they feel like they weren't a culture fit, they need a different environment, they need more challenges, they want fewer challenges, or they may no longer be interested in the idea or direction.

This doesn't mean you have to give up on your idea. It just means that it's time to reevaluate how the team is working together.

If it's a sign that there is indeed something broken in your organization, then it's time to think about how to fix it. Start by understanding why your teammate left and share the reason for their departure with the rest of your team.

I remember I once hired an intern who I thought was really promising, based on a referral. But one month in, she hadn't done anything. I talked to my marketing manager and we agreed that the intern had to be fired. However, we failed to tell the rest of the team about what happened. They found out a week later and were worried that we were just going to start firing everyone without justification. Once we sat down and explained the situation, they understood why things played out the way they did.

If you are concerned about building a team in the long term, then you want to think about how you are going to retain your teammates. You'll need to offer them training and support, have clear criteria for evaluating their progress, acknowledge their efforts and accomplishments, and be sure to celebrate key milestones. These all might seem really big or small, but at the end of the day, they make people feel valued and appreciated.

If people are motivated, they build great things!

Review

Before you start building, you want to sit down and create a roadmap so you have a sense of where you're headed. It's OK if it changes. The features you've listed in the roadmap need to be broken down into user stories. Those user stories need to be as granular as possible to avoid scope creep.

Once you have a sense for what you're building and are committed to building it, then you can recruit teammates to help you build. You decide what kind of team you're going to lead: in-house, remote, or outsourced. In any case, you need to set some clear standards for communicating.

To save you and your team time and effort, you might decide to buy a solution instead of building it in-house. This is a great option as you're getting started.

Finally, it's not enough to just recruit and build. You also need to think about how you're going to resolve conflicts, deal with departures, and keep people motivated!

Interview with Julia Grace, Head of Engineering at Tindie

Tindie[44] is the marketplace for makers to fund and sell their hardware creations. Every day it is becoming easier and cheaper to design and manufacture hardware. Small businesses around the world are popping up in industries from electronics to 3D printing. Tindie works with those businesses to bring their products to the world.[45]

I chose to interview Julia Grace because I wanted to gain the perspective of someone who runs engineering at an early-stage startup and focuses primarily on building products. As you read through the interview, you'll learn how Julia manages engineering teams, recruits technical talent, and builds products.

Poornima: "Hi Julia! Thanks for taking the time to do an interview with me today. Let's start by talking about your background. What got you into technology?"

Julia: "When I was very young (middle school age), my parents brought home an old Commodore 64. I played very rudimentary video games on it, then became curious about writing my own. I borrowed a BASIC programming book from school and the rest is history. I'd ride my bike to the library and check out additional books on programming throughout middle and high school. When I got to college, I majored in Computer Science with a focus on distributed systems at UNC [University of North Carolina Chapel Hill]."

Poornima: "Wow, it's great to hear that you've stuck to your passion all these years. What did you do after college?"

Julia: "Right after college, I worked in consulting and ended up on a project at the Supreme Court of Virginia. At the time, all criminal records were stored locally (in databases at each police station). This meant that if someone committed a crime in one county and then later in another, it would take some time before the courts figured it out. I worked on the first project that moved this system into the cloud, creating a centralized database to keep track of the criminal records online. This was way before AWS (Amazon Web Services) and other platforms that allowed for easy cloud storage."

Poornima: "That was definitely a much-needed solution."

Julia: "Yeah, it really taught me about the power of computing as it applies to other industries."

Poornima: "What did you do next?"

Julia: "I went back to grad school at UNC, and after graduating I really wanted to move to Silicon Valley. I got a job at IBM Almaden Research in San Jose, where I stayed for several years, building systems, writing papers and filing patents. Then I caught the startup bug."

Poornima: "What was your first startup and what did you do?"

Julia: "I worked at a small startup in the affiliate marketing space, VigLink, as their first product manager. After that I went to WeddingLovely (which was part of the 500 Startups accelerator), where I was the co-founder and CTO, and now I'm heading engineering at Tindie."

Poornima: "Why did you decide to go the CTO route versus building your own product?

Julia: "In a startup, there are a lot of things you have to do that have little to do with engineering (sales, marketing, etc.), and you've gotta be really heads down and get them done. But I love engineering, and I wanted to go through the process of writing and scaling up an application."

Poornima: "That makes a lot of sense. I know I decided against that role because I wanted to learn more about business."

Julia: "Yeah, but I do also really enjoy engineering leadership, helping people of all levels develop in their careers, and in particular, I like to work with other very talented engineers."

Poornima: "Now that you're running engineering at Tindie, how do you go about recruiting? Do you look for things like balancing senior and junior engineers?"

Julia: "I look for smart, passionate people who can get things done with good attention to detail. What matters most is to find people who can build and ship features and who understand that done is always better than perfect. That being said, you have to be careful that the people you're hiring are mature in their decision making to know when not to make unnecessary shortcuts. "

Poornima: "And do you mind that, say, a junior engineer may take a little more time to get up to speed?"

Julia: "It takes people different amounts of time to acclimate, and it's more important to have intuition to build. Some people take longer to develop that intuition. I've seen successful companies that have been built by people right out of college, and others built by all senior-level people."

Poornima: "And how do you go about motivating people when you have deadlines or need to rework a code base?"

Julia: "Being transparent about what's going on in the company is really important. When everyone has a general idea of the state of the business, no one is surprised when things take a turn for the worst, or the best. It also takes a great amount of emotional intelligence (so-called "EQ") to know when someone is feeling down. Sometimes employees are distracted for personal reasons, but as a boss you want to ensure they are fulfilled and challenged in their job while also respecting their privacy. I like to hold up a mirror and start with things like, 'I see that you are feeling this way...' No one can really argue with your assessment because it's your assessment, but the key is to get the other person to open up a little and self-reflect. The key is to be to be empathic but not sympathetic."

Poornima: "That is a pretty powerful technique; I've learned to use it too, and it gives people the benefit of the doubt. You acknowledge that something else is going on that is distracting them or impacting their productivity, rather than assuming they're just being slackers. I also know that a lot of engineers get demotivated by founders who change direction. How do you deal with that?"

Julia: "The person who yearns for stability isn't going to be right for a startup. You need to find people who are OK with change, but still want to work toward a big purpose. You also want to encourage your team to voice their concerns because just like you don't want to surprise them, they shouldn't surprise you. If things are going well for a particular person, you should know through having one-on-one meetings, etc."

Poornima: "Yeah, I highly recommend postmortems at least once a quarter, where people get a chance to talk about what is and isn't working for them. It doesn't mean we can resolve all the issues, but we can pick at least one or two and see if we can resolve them as a team."

Julia: "Founders also need to learn to understand what motivates the engineers they are recruiting; some people are motivated primarily by money, others by impact, others by role. After you figure out what the recruit is most passionate about, the founders then need to decide if those motivations align with the culture and values of the company."

Poornima: "Completely agree. I think people too often feel like engineers are commodities, when they are humans. They have their preferences and passions for what they want to do, and it's important to find a fit when recruiting. What about deadlines? I know a lot of people are moving away from setting hard deadlines and shipping when things are ready. What is your take on that?"

Julia: "Deadlines make you put your stick in the mud and 'rally the troops' around a common goal. People want direction, they want to know what role they are playing in the greater purpose of the company, what they are working towards and what the timeline is for them to get there. I like to focus on having internal deadlines so everyone is on the same page about what needs to be delivered when and why."

Poornima: "And what about those aggressive founders who want things done fast?"

Julia: "Founders need to understand the technical process, or at least have a general appreciation for technical work and its complexities. When giving estimates, it is very important to give them some padding while being as realistic as possible. Remember, better to under promise and over deliver than the opposite."

Poornima: "Let's switch gears now and talk a little bit about your current startup, Tindie. What was your first contribution?"

Julia: "The first version that was built was a little shaky. I rewrote large portions of it and engineers I hired did as well, under my guidance."

Poornima: "How did you prioritize technical debt and how do you deal with it going forward?"

Julia: "Taking shortcuts in the beginning is OK to get your MVP out the door and test it. Even today as we do tests we'll start with a hypothesis like, 'We think this feature will drive more sales or engagement.' If we're wrong, we rip it out. If we're right, then we need to build it out and clean up any shortcuts we've taken. Otherwise, it will be hard to maintain the code base. You don't want to have a situation where no one wants to touch portions of the code base because they are afraid of breaking it, introducing bugs, etc."

Poornima: "That's a great approach. I wish more people realized the importance of refactoring. Thanks again, Julia, for taking the time to share your approach on recruiting and heading an engineering team. I wish you and Tindie continued success!"

Just to recap, here's what we learned from Julia Grace:

1. **You can take shortcuts when you're building your MVP to test it,** but you need to revisit it later on and refactor it. The last thing you want is a fragile system, where things are constantly breaking.

2. **You want to hire people based on their ability to get things done,** rather than the number of years of experience they have under their belt. It's also important that over time they develop a good intuition for how to build something.

3. **You can keep your engineers motivated** by being transparent, acknowledging when you've noticed a change in their behavior, and giving them a chance to voice their concerns.

4. **You want to make sure there is a good fit when you are hiring an engineer.** This means understanding their motivations, rather than trying to change someone to fit your needs.

Chapter 10

Scrappy Marketing Strategies

I have a dear friend—let's call him Sam to protect his identity. Sam is so enthusiastic and full of energy that it's hard not to want to spend time with him. Years ago, Sam would "invest" in a new sport every 3 to 6 months. He'd go all-out buying the coolest gear, subscribing to magazines, and spending thousands of dollars. A couple months into the sport he would hit a learning curve, and his interest for the activity would fizzle out. Sam used to have the money to support this kind of behavior, but a few years ago, he got hit pretty hard and had to cut back. Thanks to eBay, he sold off his excess sports equipment. I introduced him to yoga, which fortunately only requires a mat!

Sam suffered from shiny object syndrome. He'd hear something was cool, go all in, and then his interest would die down. He never saw an ROI on the gear he had purchased or the initial time he had spent.

I've noticed a number of innovators with shiny object syndrome, especially when it comes to marketing their products. You might be suffering from this too if you've invested a lot of money into various marketing channels and hoped to see substantial results.

If you're running campaigns and not seeing results, I'd encourage you to turn them off right away! (Well, after you've finished reading this chapter.)

Paid advertising has its time and place, but jumping into it with no clear-cut strategy or plan will end up costing you a lot of time and money.

I want to start you off with some scrappy marketing strategies that have worked for me and the startups I've advised. Then, I'll recommend some best practices when it comes to weaving in paid advertising.

The reason I'm having you wait to pursue paid advertising is because paid advertising is really meant to be a shortcut for quickly acquiring customers. It's easy to acquire customers once you've tested out a channel and verified that the messages you're conveying resonate with them.

In this chapter, I'm going to cover 3 marketing channels that have made a dramatic impact on attracting customers to my startups and others I've worked with. I'm also going to talk about the expectations you need to set for yourself when using these channels, and why it's important to mesh the channels together in order to see substantial results.

Keep in mind that you can continue to use these channels as your product grows; they will certainly scale with your business. However, as you start to attract other customer segments, such as mainstream customers, you'll need to expand your channel selection and run another series of experiments to find the ones that they're receptive to.

I'll do a deep dive into a few strategies to get you started, but there may be other ones you consider. I highly recommend you comb through your interview data to understand which channels resonate with your customers, and if you haven't asked during the interview, then you should do so now.

No matter which marketing channel you use to promote your product, you'll need to include and test combinations of the following elements:

- Creative (e.g., the images you use)
- Messaging
- CTA (call-to-action)

The length of the creative and messaging that you use will vary across channels.

With that, let's dig into the 3 scrappy marketing channels: search, email, and social media.

Section 1

Search: How to get customers to discover your product

Organic search is a really effective approach because it attracts customers who already have a clear intent to purchase (they are actively looking for products).

To show up in organic search results, you need to do content marketing and have a site that is optimized for a web crawler.

Content marketing[46] is any marketing that involves the creation and sharing of media and publishing content in order to acquire customers. This information can be presented in a variety of formats, including news, videos, white papers, e-books, infographics, case studies, how-to guides, question and answer articles, photos, and more.

I know what you're thinking: *"Content marketing, ugh, that's so much work!"* Well, it is, depending on how you think about it. I like to think of content marketing as purely storytelling. I am telling the story of my product and the people who benefit from it.

You should think about content marketing as storytelling because stories:

- are relatable;

- capture the values of your product and company;
- can be easily repeated to others (word-of-mouth is the most powerful means of attracting customers); and
- are an authentic way of showing how your product solves a problem or provides a valuable experience.

Even after learning this, some people only talk about the how of their products (i.e., how it works through its features). While that's important, it's not the sole reason customers buy a product.

They're asking you, *"Why should I buy this product from you?"*

You have to put everything in terms that apply to your customer. I see people make a classic mistake over and over again: they just describe themselves.

- *"We're such an amazing team of experts." Meanwhile, the customer is thinking: "Why do I want to work with an amazing team of experts? Uh oh, maybe experts will be expensive..."*
- *"Our product has XYZ feature." Translation in a customer's mind: "Do I even need XYZ feature right now?"*

Customers don't want to read these descriptions. It causes them to have to make decisions, which is mentally taxing. What they want to know is how this product will benefit them. Therefore, everything needs to be developed through the lens of the customer:

- *"Our team of experts will take the time to understand your needs, and then suggest strategies that will ensure sure you project is completed on time and within budget."*

Your content marketing can tell stories by:

- Showcasing customers through case studies of how your product has benefited them.

- Demonstrating thought leadership in the form of value-added blog posts that indicate that your company has expertise related to the problems your customers face.

- Providing specific use cases to illustrate how your product can solve common problems that your customers experience.

- And, don't forget to include a single CTA at the end of a piece of content! I know that people are reluctant to tell others what to do. They want their content to linger in the minds of potential customers. Unfortunately, that's just too subtle! It's like creating a delicious meal for a dinner party and then forgetting to invite your guests to join you!

You need to invite your customers to check out your product. So, include a single CTA in each piece of content you create. Only one CTA, and not more, because giving people too much to do will overwhelm them, and then they won't do anything at all.

Here are some examples of content marketing that does a good job of telling stories.

1. MailChimp does a lot of great case studies in the form of blog posts that showcase how its customers benefit from its product.[47]

2. Another startup, Gumroad, knows the problems its customers are facing and writes blog posts that highlight solutions using other products, not just its own! You'll notice that at the end of the Gumroad post, there is a single CTA requesting the readers to enter their email addresses.[48]

Let's talk about using content to attract customers through search. The way you receive traffic to your site through content marketing is via SEO (search engine optimization). A web crawler visits your website periodically and notes how clean, relevant, timely, accessible, and fast-loading the content is. Using this information, it creates a

PageRank score for your website. That PageRank is, effectively, your "location" in the search results. The higher you rank, the more likely you are to get traffic. Search engines will only rank websites highly if they know the website is producing high-quality content. What that means is that it's not enough to just pump out a ton of content: it also has to be good. High-quality content has a low bounce rate and some initial traffic.

OK, I know what you're thinking: *"That's a Catch-22. I need traffic to get more traffic?"*

That's where cross-promotion is key, and I'll explain how to cross-promote using other channels like social media and email in the upcoming sections.

For now, let's continue talking about how we can improve your search PageRank score by making a web crawler your BFF!

What Crawlers Love

- Valid links

- Clear site structure

- Clear navigation

- HTML and CSS, because they provide static information (sites that are primarily JavaScript or AJAX are dynamic—in other words, they rely on user input.)

- Categories

- Short URLs

- Short, easy-to-remember domain names

Note that crawlers can only crawl public sites. So, if you have a lot of content behind a login wall, you won't really benefit from it.

Content marketing does require an initial investment of time before you see results, and you might feel like search engines are constantly changing their algorithms. However, if you invest in creating quality content, you will be rewarded. The reason people have lost their PageRanks in the past is because they did things like use content farms to pump out low-quality content or stuff keywords into irrelevant content. If done well, SEO and content marketing will give you a longer shelf life than other channels.

Shelf life of common marketing channels:

- A tweet: A few minutes or possibly hours, depending on the number of people someone follows on Twitter.

- An email: 7 days max!

- AdWords: Turn it off and you're history; your PageRank immediately drops off.

Here are some advanced strategies to really boost your organic rankings and keep them high:

- Perform a periodic SEO audit.[49]

- Check out a tool like OpenSite Explorer[50] to keep track of who is linking to you, who is linking to your competitor, and searching for broken links.[50]

Exercise 10.1: Create a post about your product.

Objective: Practice creating high-value posts that educate your potential customer on what you do. Here are a couple examples of posts I've created in the past.

- "Journey from Founding Engineer to Founder"[51]

- "Innovators: Is your head filled with questions?"[52]

Directions:

1. Start with a story that ties into the theme of what you're going to talk about. You can tell a story about a customer like I did in my first example, or a personal experience you had. Just make sure the story is short and highly relevant.

2. Figure out what you're trying to sell and create bullet points around the benefits.

3. Include a CTA (call-to-action) at the end telling people what to do (e.g., learn more, sign up for your product, or buy it).

I know a lot of people are reluctant to tell their readers what to do. But you need to think about it more in terms of taking away the strenuous decision-making process for them. Remember, these people are coming to you for a solution or an experience! If you truly believe in your product and have managed to convince the customer of its benefits, then it's very likely they are a good fit. But you need to get them to do that last step, which is to make a purchasing decision!

Exercise 10.2: Create a case study blog post.

Objective: Showcase existing or potential customers.

Here are some examples of case studies. The first is a blog post that has a very compelling story and a clear call-to-action. While it doesn't feature a software product, I'm including it because it's got the right format. The second example shows how AirBnB does a great job of humanizing its product with captivating stories, and the call-to-action is to share them.

- Nathan Barry's case study promoting Authority: "How Samuel Hulick made over $37,000 with his self-published book"[53]
- AirBnB stories[54]

Even if you don't have customers yet, you can still reach out to people and showcase them. Here's an example of how we showcased a private instructor for BizeeBee:

- "Victoria Klein: Making Yoga More Accessible"[55]

In this case, we didn't include a call-to-action, because we just cared about building general awareness. However, we do allude to the fact that BizeeBee can help Victoria with her business.

Directions:

1. If you've already got customers, reach out and interview them about how they use your product. The conversation you'll have needs to revolve around what their life was like before your product, and how it has changed dramatically since then.

2. If you don't have customers yet, find people who fit the profile of your ideal customer and showcase them. Your goal is to discover what's unique about them that your readers will find relatable and engaging.

3. Once you're done with your conversation, write it up. Let the person whom you've interviewed know about the write-up so they can share it too!

The content you create is going to lead potential customers to your site through organic search and some cross-promotion, which we'll get to shortly. While search will lead customers who have a clear intent to purchase straight to your website, it's not the best channel when it comes to closing customers, because it relies on the fleeting moments of an initial website visit to convince customers to purchase. Most customers are window shoppers. They're going to visit your website, check out your product, and then either decide to purchase or defer their decision to a later time. If they're not ready, then you've just lost the lead and the sale!

Ideally, you want to drive potential customers to your site and then ask interested visitors for their contact info so you can follow up with them periodically. The way to do this is to set up an email capture form on your website, then leverage email marketing to continue the conversation and eventually close them.

If you don't have a website or a landing page set up yet, you'll need to do that first. Here's an example of an early Mint.com landing page.

Figure 10.1 An early landing page for Mint.com.

Now it's your turn to create a landing page!

Exercise 10.3: Set up a landing page.

Objective: Create a landing page with a clear value proposition.

Directions:

Here are a couple tools I recommend using to create your landing page:

- LaunchRock:[56] This product is great because it's super simple to use. I highly recommend it for setting up a "Coming Soon!" page.

- Unbounce:[57] If you have multiple personas and value propositions you want to test, then use this product.

- Start with the copy. Don't get too worried yet about how your landing page is going to look and what imagery it will use. We'll get to that shortly! I want you to start by resurrecting those value propositions from Chapter 8 Exercise 8.1.

  Recall that the **value proposition** is the customer's end goal, achieved by using your product.

  You'll need to have a compelling headline that makes it clear who this product is for and then follow it by listing out benefits. You need to answer the question: *how does your product help your customer* (NOT what features does it have)?

- Pick a simple image that complements your value proposition. The more authentic and relatable you can make it, the better. Check out iStockphoto[58] if you're looking for images.

- A call-to-action (CTA) such as an email capture.

  When it comes to CTAs, you need to think about what you want people to do right when they come to your website.

  Ideally, you will only have 1 CTA per page. If you have too many, people will do things you really don't want them to do—or, they'll be confused and do nothing!

  Since you're probably building up a list of early adopters, I'm going to recommend that you make your main CTA an email capture (I'll show you how to set that up in the next exercise).

- Include trust indicators. If you already have customers, you can include a short testimonial. If you don't, then put in a link to an About page describing your team (at the bottom so that it doesn't interfere with the call-to-action), or something else that humanizes the site. Otherwise, people will think that you're going to spam them.

You might have heard about A/B testing your landing page copy to understand which value proposition resonates with your customers. I'll dig into A/B testing in Chapter 12.

Maybe you're not yet convinced that email can close customers. By the end of the next section, you will be!

Section 2

Why email is the most effective channel for converting customers

The reason we think email isn't an effective channel is because each one of us suffers from inbox clutter. Even though you get a lot of emails, you probably still feel obligated to go through each email to make sure you're not missing some important communication, especially if it's from someone you were expecting to hear from.

The truth is email is the most targeted communication channel. Nearly $2.1B is spent on email marketing annually.

Everything matters in an email: delivery time, subject, sender, and the message contained within it. However, people gloss over these details and conclude that email is ineffective.

Before we dive into the email and campaigns, let's take a step back and talk about how to build up your list!

If you've set up content marketing and are driving potential customers to your website, then you'll want to be sure to include an email capture form on each post like I mentioned in the previous section, as well as make it the single CTA on all your landing pages.

You might be thinking, *"Why not just get them to purchase right now?"* Or, *"Why not just drive them to a pricing page?"*

You can do that if you have already launched your product, because then they can sign up and while they're doing so, you can ask for their email. But, if you don't have anything for them to purchase yet, then you'll still want to capture the lead.

I'm going to cover price testing in a future chapter, so just sit tight!

You might still be worried that you won't capture any emails. Well, I can assure you that you won't get any if you don't have a way to capture them. And you'll only see a trickle if you don't have a clear value proposition and list out the benefits. This is why it's really important that you take the time to test out messaging through content marketing.

Here are a couple tools I recommend using to create email capture forms:

- MailChimp:[59] I love this tool and probably use it at least a few times a week. I personally think it's one of the easiest to use on the market, and believe me, I've had my fair share of wrestling with email campaign management software. Their pricing is also pretty fair and affordable. They also provide a lot of helpful tutorials, including one on setting up your own email capture forms.[60]

- ConvertKit:[61] If you want more flexibility in creating forms and changing their design, or plan to do a freebie or giveaway as part of signing up for a list, then I'd recommend using ConvertKit. I attended Nathan Barry's ConvertKit Academy and found it useful for selling info products.

I know that many people prefer to use something like Google Forms to capture email addresses. I figure they're doing this because MailChimp and many other email tools use a double opt-in—which requires that customers confirm subscription by clicking a link in their email—and they're worried this will cause drop-off. However, here are some reasons to do the double opt-in instead of using Google Forms:

1. **You'll potentially lose leads.** People are notorious for "fat-fingering" their email addresses! You want to make sure the email address that you capture is valid. Once you capture the email, you need to take them to a page that says something like "please check your email and click to confirm."

2. **People will forget that they signed up for your service, and when you send them an email later, they will flag you as a spammer.** You might as well walk them through the validation step right now to make sure the customer is really interested.

3. **People have grown to accept some form of validation.** Many expect to get something in their inboxes immediately.

Finally, be sure to test the signup process yourself, and test the experience on mobile! I learned that from teaching my course. One of the students pointed out that the mobile experience was horrible. I thought he was the only one using mobile, but I went into MailChimp and looked at the data. Sure enough, nearly 30% of subscribers were reading my lessons on their mobile devices (in case you're curious, 26% of them were on iOS). So, I changed the layout to be more mobile friendly. Yet another lesson demonstrating how data drives decisions!

Types of email you want to send out

Once you've set up your email capture form, it's time to start sending emails. Do not think that your list is too small to start sending out emails. Instead, realize that people gave you their email addresses and are waiting to hear from you! The sooner you start sending out valuable information and the more frequently you do it, the more likely someone is to forward your info to another potential customer (once again, the power of word-of-mouth marketing).

When I say this, I know people get really nervous and are afraid that if they send out emails frequently, they'll be perceived as *spammy*.

Here's the thing: if people don't want your emails they can unsubscribe at any time. It's a clear signal that they really weren't interested. However, if they are interested, they'll want to hear from you, and they'll stay subscribed.

To keep people on your email list engaged, you'll want to make sure the message is personalized and relevant.

Here are the types of email campaigns to send out and their email frequency:

Drip campaign

The goal of a drip campaign is to periodically send out valuable information. Valuable information does not mean a sales pitch! It means helpful guidance and insights like how to use your product, how to get in touch with your company for customer support, or solutions to problems that customers might be experiencing.

You want to keep the time interval consistent, because the point of a drip campaign is to set the expectation that they will receive information from you daily, weekly, or monthly.

For example, you might have an onboarding drip campaign that is 7 days long, and each day the customer receives an email that explains how to use different features within your product. After that, you might switch them to a weekly drip campaign in which they receive an email from you each week that shares your expertise on the types of problems they are experiencing.

You can also do a drip campaign leading up to the launch of your product or an event that you're hosting.

The goals of a drip campaign are to add value to customers' lives and use that contribution to keep people engaged and stay top-of-mind.

Here are a couple examples taken from the 5-day onboarding drip campaign from email service provider MadMimi.

Sales campaign

You're really only going to send out sales campaigns when you're running a promotion or sale. That will most likely be once per quarter or biannually.

What you don't want to do is wait until the day of a sale to send out its promotion email. Why? Because people need to be primed! What if they are on vacation and miss out on your sale?

To avoid that situation, send out a series of emails—just one per week is good enough—to prime them. Send out a final email with a CTA encouraging them to purchase on the day of the sale, and let them know that this is the last email of the sale.

Don't be afraid of sending out sales emails alongside a drip campaign. It's actually a great strategy because you're adding value and then making a small ask.

When I ran a pre-order campaign for this book, I sent out an email lesson on Thursday each week, and for 4 consecutive weeks I'd send out a reminder email about the upcoming pre-order special.

Guess how many people unsubscribed? 10. Out of a list of 450 people, that is pretty good!

Newsletter

This type of email will contain general information about product and company updates, and can be sent out monthly or quarterly.

Too often, people jam-pack newsletters with a lot of information and too many CTAs. If you find yourself putting sales or product info into a newsletter, then move that info into either a drip or sales campaign.

They lead by example: have a nice banner.

Highlight the day.

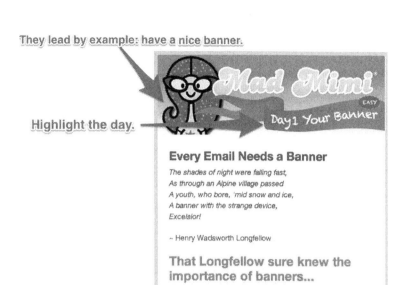

Figure 10.2 First day drip email.

Signpost the day and theme.

Starting with a story.

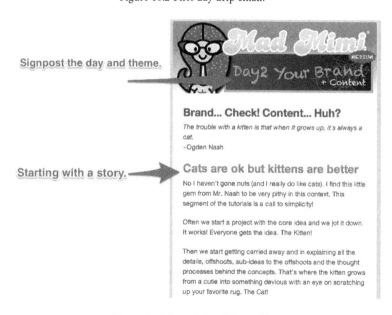

Figure 10.3 Second day drip email.

Lifecycle campaigns

These are campaigns you send out to pull customers back into your product, and they are triggered based off of customers' actions (or inaction).

The goal of these campaigns is to increase engagement with your customers and stay top-of-mind. To set a campaign up like this, you'd need to use a tool like Mixpanel.[62]

So now you're probably wondering, *"How is email effective at converting customers?"*

Let's take a top-down view. You are pulling leads in through your landing page, nurturing them through a drip campaign, and then priming them through a sales campaign with a single CTA to purchase. Yes, it might be a lot of steps, but honestly, it takes people a while to get interested and invested in your product and company.

The reason email is effective is because you've gotten the invitation into their inbox; there's no other medium that lets you do this without being intrusive. Think about it: when you call someone, you might catch them at a bad time. If you show up unannounced, there's also an issue with timing. But with email, if they have subscribed, then they've indicated that they are waiting to hear from you! You just have to make sure that you're telling them things that are worthwhile. Therefore, you'll have to manage the ratio of value-add to ask. I'm not going to sit here and tell you it's 80/20. You've gotta test it out. Keep track of your unsubscribe rate from the start; it will signal fit or disinterest.

Finally, you can cross-promote content. If you write a blog post that you think is worth sharing with your subscribers, send them the first few paragraphs in an email with a link to come to your blog and read the rest. This will also clearly signal whether or not your audience members are truly interested in your product.

Exercise 10.4: Create a drip campaign.

Objective: Creating a drip campaign to stay engaged with your customers and potential customers.

Directions:

1. You can send out a drip campaign that onboards your customer onto your product (if it's built or being built). Or, you can send one that conveys the benefits of your product (highlight one benefit per email).

2. Create 3-5 emails.

3. Include 1 CTA. Yup, that's right—just like a landing page or blog post, your emails also need to have a CTA! You can post a question that you want them to answer, or direct them to sign up for your product.

4. Schedule the emails to go out on a consistent time interval: daily, weekly, or monthly.

5. Remember to keep track of subscribe and unsubscribe rates to see what messaging is working.

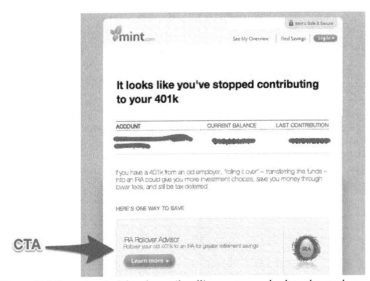

Figure 10.4 Example of a lifecycle email pulling customers back to the product

Section 4

If your customers are social, then invest in social media

People jump into social media thinking that it will be a silver bullet, and when they don't see results (e.g., revenue), they end up blaming the channel.

Just like search or content marketing, social media marketing is a way to get leads, but it is not a way to close them! Once again, save that for email.

Also, if you are going to use social media, please make sure that your customers are using it too! I've noticed a number of times people use it and complain that their customers aren't on Facebook, Pinterest, Twitter, or YouTube. Well, if they aren't there, then don't bother.

No one is telling you that you have to use social media!

If you do know your potential customers are hanging out on social media, that's great. The purpose of social media is to give you the ability to reach anyone that you're allowed to follow. But understand your customers' affinities to particular networks and concentrate on those. If you take a broad approach, you'll end up wasting a lot of time and energy. So, if you cannot follow your potential customers on a network, skip it!

The ultimate goal is to have people follow you back, and once that happens, you can start to build awareness through casual conversations.

Unfortunately, most people make the mistake of just posting rather than pulling people into conversations. This creates a one-way street and you just end up talking at customers.

If you want to effectively convert people, you have to incite interest through a conversation and then drive them to an action like reading a blog post or going to a landing page to find out more info.

Don't just create content constantly— cross-promote it!

Back in 2011, I asked a BizeeBee customer, Mark, how he heard about us and why he decided to sign up. He said he had seen us on Facebook and signed up for our email newsletter, but it wasn't until he received a postcard from us that he signed up.

It took 3 touchpoints to get Mark to convert, but I've actually seen it take more, sometimes up to 7!

The reason I'm bringing this up is because you have to be a little bit patient with customers and you also have to send them messages on a few different mediums. When you're just getting started, you don't know which message is going to resonate with the customer or on what medium. Eventually you will find out by keeping track of the metrics, which I'll talk about in Chapter 12.

It might feel like you have to keep creating a lot of content, ads, and landing pages, but you don't. What you want to do is cross-promote.

Just because you write a blog post, doesn't mean that it just has to sit on your blog. You can take the post and put it into an email, or share the link to it across social media channels.

Yes, you're saying the same thing across a number of channels, but sometimes your customers need to hear and see a message multiple times in different places before they take action.

Review

Start with the scrappy marketing strategies: content marketing, email, and social media are a great way to test whether your message resonates with your customers. You'll want to set expectations for yourself by recognizing what channels are designed to do. Some are great at just pulling in leads (content marketing and social media), while others are great for nurturing and closing customers (email).

You should also consider promoting across each channel without worrying that you're saying the same thing! People often have channels that they're more receptive to than others, but it's really about hearing the message a few times before it sinks in and compels them to take action.

If you didn't ask your customers what channels they are using in your initial interviews, now is a good time to do so!

Finally, realize that many of the channels I've reviewed are great for attracting early adopters. You can continue to use them as you scale, but as you look for more mainstream customers, you'll have to explore new channels and run more experiments to test whether your messaging and CTA attracts them to your product.

 Chapter 11

How to ASK for Your First Dollar

In 2005 I was buying my first car ever. It was one year after I graduated from college, so I was on a really tight budget. I thought about buying a used car, but it turns out the interest rate for financing a used vehicle is much higher than the rate available for a brand new one. I continued to do research and ultimately came up with a price ceiling of $15,000. However, I knew that the cost of ownership would actually include monthly payments for the car, insurance, gas, and occasional tune-ups. So in the end, I'd probably be paying slightly more overall—something like $17,000. And then there's the issue of a car being a depreciating asset ... I'd just have to deal with that.

Once I set my price ceiling, I was on the hunt for a dealer who would meet this figure or come as close to it as possible.

I happened to stumble upon the one car salesman who wanted to go out of his way to ensure that I had a really good experience. He picked me up from work around 5pm and took me to the dealership. We did the usual: picked out a color and model, then went for a test drive.

Once we were done with the test drive, I thanked him for his time and said I'd need to think it over. But of course, being the awesome car salesman he was, he wouldn't let me go without completing the sale. He said, *"This car won't be available tomorrow ... If you want it, you'll need to buy it tonight."*

I didn't want to appear too desperate, and I told him, *"Make it $15,000 and you've got a deal."* At this point, I had laid all my cards out on the table, and figured that I was probably making some newbie negotiator faux pas.

He said, "DEAL!"

Whew.

That was only the start of the process. He walked me over to the finance department where I had to undergo a credit check process, fill out tons of paperwork, and pay a down payment (probably the biggest check I'd written at that point in my life). It was nearly midnight when we completed the sale and I got to drive home in my shiny new car!

The interesting thing about car sales is that manufacturers and dealers work hard to position each type of car they sell in terms of quality and status. Of course, they neglect to inform you about total cost of ownership, because they know that it's someone else's problem: the car insurance company, the car mechanic, the parts manufacturer—the list goes on. Manufacturers and dealers couldn't care less about that stuff. Instead, they focus on selling you on the value of driving their particular brand of car, knowing that you have a very pressing need: to get to work on time to pay the car bill!

You'll need to think in similar terms as you consider pricing your product, and we'll dig into how to go about doing that in this chapter.

Section 1

What is pricing?

Pricing is the perceived value of your product, which means that it's more than just a figure. In my example above, I perceived the value of a car to be transportation, and to me that should be around $15,000.

Much of the perceived value circles back to **positioning**. Remember, positioning is creating an image or identity in the minds of the target market. Occupy a position in a prospective customer's mind—

one that reflects strengths and weaknesses as well as those of the competitor.

It ultimately determines the type of customers you attract, and determines the type of customers you eliminate.

I was a customer who was attracted to a low-end starter car, and I knew what I wanted down to the make and model!

To price your product, the first goal is to arrive as close to a reservation price as possible. A reservation price is the price at which a customer feels a little pinch, but they are in such great need that they are willing to pay for it.

At this point in time, we're not going to focus on how to optimize for revenue, but do know that you can always change your price and your **pricing model**. Your pricing model is how you go about collecting payment from customers. In my car purchase example, the pricing model was monthly financing with a 1% down payment and 1% interest.

There are a number of models out there. Here are some to think about—they're the most commonly used for software products:

- Freemium: Offer a product with limited features for free, then make the customer pay to use more features.

- Monthly Subscription: Bill them a set price once a month.

- Transaction Fee: Take a percentage-based fee of whatever someone is purchasing. Most commonly used by marketplaces, it's thought of as a convenience fee.

- In-App Purchases: Get people to purchase virtual goods within a mobile application.

- App Purchase: Get people to pay for your mobile application when they download it. Usually, customers are given the choice between a free mobile app with limited features and a feature-rich app they need to pay for.

- Metered: Charge users based on the volume of something (e.g., number of text messages or emails sent out using your product).

- Licensing: Charge per user.

- Advertising: Charge people to advertise on your site with a banner or display ad.

- Sponsorships: Charge people to sponsor your product.

- Revenue Share: Charge people only when they get paid, if your product helps them make money.

Pricing is not about your comfort level. It's about the customer's willingness to pay $X.

Section 2

Why should you price your product?

One of your goals might be to build a product and then transform it into a business. If that is indeed the goal, then you're going to need to cover the cost of running a business, hence you need to charge people for your product.

The second reason you should charge is because you'll get a better understanding of your customers and what they value in your product.

I cannot tell you how many people I have come across who just give away their products because they feel like it's still in beta or a prototype. As a result, they have no idea what their customers value in it.

When you put a price on your product, customers provide feedback, and that in turn helps direct what gets built.

Section 3

When do you price?

Once you have a hypothesis of who your customers are, that's when you price.

Notice that I didn't say you should price when you have a finished or polished product, or when you have a prototype.

You want to price early and even before the product is built! The point is to test price early and often in order to figure out the bounds of what your customers are willing to pay.

This isn't about being greedy. It's about figuring out what is going to sustain your business, covering the cost of things like servicing customers and scaling growth.

Section 4

How NOT to price

Directly asking a customer what price you should charge doesn't help, because it doesn't get at the value they are deriving from a product.

Nor does it make sense to set up a series of price points and ask a question like, "Would you buy this at $X, $Y, or $Z?" This makes the customer think you're negotiating with them.

Finally, I know a lot of people do feature-based pricing, and you can too if you'd like. **Feature-based pricing** is when you offer various price points (low to high), and offer one or more features at the various price points. I personally feel like you end up leaving money on the table, because it doesn't capture the entire value of what you are offering, such as quality and customer service, which goes beyond the product itself. Customers need to know and understand the value of that too.

Section 5

How should you price?

You want to first start by understanding the ROI (return on investment) that customers are looking for.

For example, when I was price testing with BizeeBee, I knew that people were losing money on expired memberships, and that was a pretty big problem. So I'd ask them, *"Do you know how much money you're losing each month?"* Some people knew and many didn't, but they gave me a ballpark estimate of around $100+.

As a follow up, I asked if they'd be willing to pay for a product that was around $100 if it could help them recoup those expired membership fees.

Most said no, and when I followed up I discovered that the reason they wouldn't pay $100 is because it would only address a single problem: *loss of revenue.* They wanted more than that. They also wanted to grow their topline revenues by doing things like getting their first-time customers to come back and upgrade their memberships. Finally, we were getting somewhere!

I started to understand the value they were looking for from a product, partly in terms of what it could do, but also in terms of what they needed.

A second approach is to understand **substitutes** (i.e., other products they are currently using), and explore their limitations.

With BizeeBee customers, I discovered that many people were using Excel or some form of free spreadsheets. So I'd ask them, *"What do you do when you need to share your data with your accountant? What happens if your studio floods or your computer gets stolen?"* They hadn't thought about those situations. Maybe backing up their data using a service in the cloud would be prudent and worth paying for!

Realize that if your product is in a particular category, there may be a price floor and ceiling. Luxury goods have a **price floor**, and if you try to price below it, people will question the value of the product. Non-luxury products have **price ceilings** that are often set by competitors and reinforced if the market is crowded.

I mentioned above that customers need to understand that your pricing is not just about the product but the experience too, and they should be including that in their ROI.

This is known as **value pricing**.

It's up to you to figure out what the customer values, make sure those values are evident to them, and then translate that into an amount they are willing to pay for.

Time, convenience, and exclusivity (to convey status or a persona) are things that people value. However, some are more likely to put a higher or lower price on each of these things.

Another type of pricing is known as **impact pricing**, which is basically answering the question, *"How easy is it to pay?"* Amazon's

1-click is the best example, because it appeals to people's desire for instant gratification: *"I gotta have it now!"*

Offering financing options is another form of impact pricing, because you make the product more affordable to them by changing its value. Tesla Motors does this. A Tesla model S is $100K—who can afford that? Well, probably the wealthy 1%, but that's such a small market! Most luxury car purchasers gravitate toward buying BMWs, Mercedes, Lexus, and Audis that are about $50K. In an attempt to attract those buyers, Tesla found that they could get those same customers by offering a 5-year financing option instead of the traditional 3-year financing option. The reason this appealed to customers was because their monthly payments (all they really cared about) would stay the same; they'd be paying for a longer time, but they'd have the bonus of a higher status.

In addition to impact pricing you want to consider *payment models* such as layaway, loss leaders (giving something small away for free to get people interested), and upsell opportunities.

However, I will advise you to pick one approach because ultimately customers want a simple option that they can wrap their heads around.

Discounting

In general, I am not a fan of discounting when it comes to getting customers in the door. I think it attracts a certain type of customer—one who demands a lot and drives up the cost of servicing them! They are not profitable customers.

However, I do believe in providing discounts as an incentive or a reward for loyal customers!

For example, at BizeeBee I've raised prices a number of times, but I don't change it for existing customers. Instead, I let them stay at their current price, and request that they pre-pay for a whole year to lock in the rate. Since they've been around and value the product, I know they are willing to pre-pay. I'm also recognizing that they have been loyal customers and want to encourage them to stick around, so I don't want to raise prices on them unless I'm offering something brand new.

Section 6

How much time do customers need to make a decision?

People get really bogged down by thinking about how much they'll charge and forget that the price they set will also affect the amount of time a prospective customer takes to make a purchase!

This is what I like to call **buy time**. Think about it this way: how much time does it take you to decide to buy a pack of gum? Probably around 60 seconds, and most of that time is probably spent picking out a flavor, not spent asking yourself, "Do I want gum?" But when it comes to things like buying a plane ticket, you shop around. Or, if it's a big-ticket item like a car, you do research.

Hence, it's not enough to just price your product; you also need to understand the buy time, the behaviors that surround it, and be a part of each of those behaviors.

You can, of course, reduce the buy time with 3 things: scarcity, urgency, and exclusivity. But once again, you'll need to make sure your customers are aware of those factors as they relate to your product.

Finally, note that it's OK to change your pricing model. The reason you perform price tests is to experiment and discover what doesn't work and what does appeal to customers.

Exercise 11.1: Price your product.

Objective: Come up with a price point for your product and ASK your customers to pay that price.

Directions:

Just as you did an interview to find out the needs of your customers, you'll want to figure out how customers translate the benefits of your product into a value. By "value" I mean an amount of money they are willing to pay.

1. Pinpoint the ROI (return on investment) of your product.

    ROI is easier for products that are tools, like cars. I'm willing to pay $15,000 for a car. I think of it as an investment because I'm going to drive it to work to make more than $15,000.

    However, you can't always get a clear ROI. So you need to understand what your customer gets out of your product in terms of value. Are they interested in your product because it provides a convenience or alleviates a pain?

    If it's a convenience, what amount would they be willing to pay for it? If they're in pain, how much money does their pain cost them today?

2. Ask them about the substitutes they are currently using and how much each of those cost.

    This will help you know what their budget is. You can also come right out and ask them, but sometimes people are unwilling to divulge that information.

For example, with BizeeBee, yoga studio owners told me they were paying a personal assistant \$10/hour to do about 2 hours of manual data entry every day. I did a quick calculation: 2 hours x 5 days a week x \$10/hour = \$100.

Hence, I knew what their current budget was. My product would reduce the data entry cost, plus more.

When you go down the path of exposing substitutes that aren't necessarily getting the job done, do keep in mind that customers are going to be thinking about **switching costs:** how much time or money they will have to invest into a new product versus how much they are losing with the current product. The switching cost has to be low; otherwise, they won't be willing to part with their current product.

3. Create a pricing model.

    Once you've arrived at the price point, you want to figure out which of the models I talked about earlier in the chapter makes sense for your customers. Try to incorporate impact pricing into your pricing model.

    A common example of impact pricing is getting customers to pre-pay for several months in advance, giving them a discount if they do.

    Here's an example from Olark.

Figure 11.1 Olark's pricing tiers.

4. Once you arrive at a price point and price model through conversations, it's time to ASK for a payment!

They've already told you what they are willing to pay, so asking is actually easier than you think. If possible, push them to pre-pay; you don't need to wait until launch day.

I had 3 paying customers before launch day for BizeeBee, and they each paid $27 (their first month's bill). I asked for the money upfront (about 1-2 weeks before the launch), and they were willing to pay it.

5. Include the pricing on your product's website.

The reason I'm pushing for you to price your product and ASK customers to pay is because it'll reveal who is actually going to be a customer, and who might still be on the fence. For the latter group, note any objections they have to the price and identify what is really holding them back. Over time, you'll be able to address those concerns and objections as you continue to build your product and refine your messaging.

You'll also want to make a note of those who do pay you, their buy time, and the value they see in your product, which got them to pre-pay. The value is what you'll want others to see as well—make sure it's highlighted in all your current marketing copy. Remember Chapter 10 Exercise 10.2 on creating a case study blog post? Now you have an excellent case study customer!

Review

Pricing is based on the perceived value of your product, which is highly dependent on how you position it.

As you think about pricing for your product, you want to price test early, even before the product exists! To do that effectively, you need to understand the value and benefits your customers are looking for. If you don't know what they value, having conversations will draw those values out.

Ultimately, you want to arrive at a price point and a pricing model that is value based. Depending on how high it is, you'll need to spend time educating your customers and being a part of their buy time.

What you've validated in this chapter

If you completed the exercise in this chapter then you should have validated the following:

- A price point that your customers are willing to pay for your product even before it has been built.

- The amount of time it takes for a customer to pay for your product, known as buy time.

Chapter 12

Metrics that Matter

My freshman year of college, I, like most other college newcomers, gained the "freshman 15." You know, the 15 pounds you gain because you drink beer, eat pizza at 3 a.m., and are stressed about your grades, which causes you to eat donuts, candy, and anything with lots of sugar!

I was OK with gaining some weight because I had been pretty skinny and people were giving me grief about it.

Still, I felt really self-conscious about gaining 15 pounds, and I thought losing 5 to 10 pounds would be ideal.

Then someone told me that 1 pound was equal to 3,600 calories, and to lose weight I needed to reduce the amount of calories I took in accordingly.

Made sense to me! I tried calorie counting for a week.

I lost 1 pound, and I thought, *"20% there, 4 more weeks to go!"*

The next week I jumped on the scale, but I was the same weight! The following week it was still the same, *grrrr...*

I figured I needed to cut more calories, but I just couldn't. I was hungry all the freakin' time, and I *loved* food—I still do. The more I cut, the more I craved!

Adding the stress of losing weight to the pressures of general freshman life and getting good grades wasn't fun.

I took a step back and asked myself: *"What do I really want to accomplish here?"*

So I wrote down 2 goals:

- I wanted to drop 1 dress size

- I wanted to have energy to study and spend time with my friends

I didn't set a deadline because I knew that there wasn't some magic formula for how quickly I'd be able to hit my goals. However, I did come up with a list of activities to help me accomplish my goals, such as hitting the gym and avoiding the vending machines for my meals.

Over the course of 6 months I slowly began to notice my body was changing for the better. I had more energy to focus and eventually I went down a dress size.

OK, you're probably wondering, *"What does weight loss have to do with building a product?"*

Everything!

Stepping on the scale and tracking my dress size were the analytics I needed to understand whether I was reaching my goals.

Section 1

What are metrics and analytics?

In business, analytics is the discovery and communication of meaningful patterns in data.

Based on my weight data, I decided to come up with a metric: lose 15 pounds.

A metric is measurement that is used to gauge some quantifiable component of a company's performance, such as ROI or churn rate.

However, I had come up with a **vanity metric** (pun intended) instead of a good metric: something that is comparable, understandable, and based on a rate or ratio.

Why was losing 15 pounds a vanity metric?

It didn't really signify anything about my health or well being; I could be skinny and still be unhealthy.

Instead of focusing on this vanity metric, I decided to set some higher-level goals and then think of the activities that would help me accomplish them. Dress size might still seem like a vanity metric, but here's why it's not:

1. Dress size = waistline. The waistline is a health indicator. A little belly fat is OK, but too much can lead to health problems. Hence, the act of *dropping a dress size* serves as an indicator that I am pursuing a healthy waistline for my body size.

2. My weight could still fluctuate by a few pounds on a daily basis, and that would be OK.

Similarly, in business, people seem to think that they should set a lot of metrics and proceed to optimize each one at the same time. Problems start to arise when metrics aren't tied to goals. People just see a number they have to hit, but not why that number is important. When they don't understand why, they don't know how to make decisions and eventually lose motivation. Tying a metric to a goal makes it understandable, and people will naturally start to prioritize their activities to accomplish it (i.e., they'll know how and why they need to make decisions).

When you have too many goals, they have a way of competing with one another. They compete because you have limited resources—time, capital, and talent—that you can utilize to accomplish them.

It's better to set 1 to 2 goals than 3 to 5 goals. Once you've set them, think about a small set of activities you can pursue to see if you hit them.

Next, you've got to make sure that the time interval you're setting to accomplish these goals is realistic—and by that I mean sustainable—because you want repeatable results.

It wouldn't make sense for me to starve and drop 10 pounds; my life would suck, and I'd probably just gain it back immediately. You know the type: yo-yo dieters!

The same thing happens in business, and if you don't believe me, think of all the fad products that used to exist 10 years ago but don't anymore. Those people set aggressive time intervals, probably did a ton of infomercials, hit their numbers, and went under! (Yes, I know, a few might have been lucky enough to cash out, but don't bank on that happening to you; those are some pretty slim odds.)

Finally, if something isn't working, like calorie counting, you've got to rethink your approach to hitting that goal.

If you don't want to be a yo-yo, you've got to follow this formula:

1 to 2 business goals + 1 metric + activities (which are subject to change depending on the results you see) + realistic time interval

KPIs (key performance indicators) are metrics that tie back to business goals and tell you if you are indeed accomplishing them.

Section 2

Why do we need analytics and metrics?

There is a lot of uncertainty involved with creating a new product and bringing it to market. It requires us to conduct a series of experiments.

As we're conducting experiments, we need to know if they are producing valuable results, so we need to take measurements and set metrics.

A good metric is one that is the following:

1. Comparative

2. Understandable

3. Based on a ratio or rate

In order to hit a metric goal, we make decisions that are sometimes based on data we collect. But at times, we aren't able to piece together a coherent story from just looking at data. Therefore, we need to bridge the gap between **quantitative measurements** (data) and **qualitative measurements** (which feed into stories).

For example, when I started BizeeBee I noticed that people would often sign up for the free plan, use it for a couple days, then leave. They'd return a few weeks later and log in, but they still wouldn't upgrade.

I couldn't understand this type of behavior. So I picked up the phone to call a number of them and ask why they were just logging in periodically when most customers use the product daily. They responded that they hadn't yet opened up their studio. They were testing us out, and were sharing an account with their business partner. It finally started to make sense! However, I would have never guessed this behavior just from looking at the analytics. I needed to have a conversation to really understand what was going on.

Section 3

Methods for collecting data

There are a number of ways to collect data. I'm going to mainly focus on 3 types in this book:

- Cohort Analysis

- A/B Testing

- Multivariate Testing

Cohort Analysis

	January	February	March	April	May
Total Customers	1000	1000	1000	1000	1000
Avg. Revenue Per Customer	$5.00	$4.50	$4.33	$4.25	$4.50

Figure 12.1[63] Average revenue for 5 months.

Just looking at this table really doesn't tell us much about our customers or why the average revenue is going up and down as we add customers.

	January	February	March	April	May
New Users	1000	1000	1000	1000	1000
Total Users	1000	2000	3000	4000	5000
Month 1	$5.00	$3.00	$2.00	$1.00	$0.50
Month 2		$6.00	$4.00	$2.00	$1.00
Month 3			$7.00	$6.00	$5.00
Month 4				$8.00	$7.00
Month 5					$9.00

Figure 12.2[64] Comparing revenues by the month customer arrived.

However, if we organize customers into cohorts, we start to notice patterns. We see that customers who arrived in Month 5 are spending $9 in their first month. Hence, initial spending is going up as we add features and refine the product, but we'll have to see if the trend continues.

A/B Testing

If you aren't sure of something—for example, which value proposition to put on a landing page—then you perform what's known as an A/B test. I mentioned doing this in Chapter 10 as you were creating your landing page. In an A/B test you have two groups: Group A, which is shown one version of the landing page, and Group B, which is shown another version. You then set the metric you care about—such as conversion rate or signups—and compare the results from Group A versus Group B to determine which version to go with.

You can, of course, do this type of version testing for email campaigns, features, ads, and other marketing.

To do A/B testing in emails, your email marketing tool should have an A/B testing feature that you can enable. Similarly, the tool you're using to create a landing page should also have a way to create and run an A/B test.

Multivariate Testing

This is just like A/B testing, but now you're testing multiple variables. For example, with A/B testing, you will test just a single variable like a subject line in an email; but if you want to test other things like subject, time sent, and email body copy, each of those are different variables that you are testing as well.

While I advise that you set 1-2 business goals and have a metric that helps you to measure the progress of each goal, you will want to keep an eye out for additional metrics related to marketing, product, customer, and pricing. We'll cover these in a moment.

Metrics Framework

There are a number of frameworks out there for metrics. The two most popular are Eric Ries' *"Engines of Growth"* from The Lean Startup and Dave McClure's *"Pirate Metrics."*

In Ries' framework you begin by creating a **sticky engine**, which basically tries to retain as many customers as possible. This requires changing the product to make sure it is engaging for customers. Once you have established that, you move on to determine the **virality engine** by measuring the **viral coefficient**, which is the number of new users that each user brings in (i.e., refers). You also factor in churn and loss. Finally, you create a **paid engine** that brings in payments and you measure the **customer lifetime value** (CLV) and **customer acquisition cost** (CAC).

Let's contrast this with McClure's "Pirate Metrics," which is a simple funnel consisting of the following steps: acquisition, activation, retention, revenue, and referral. At each step of the funnel you will experience a loss of customers.

In both of these, the end goal is the same: get paying customers through word-of-mouth marketing (referrals).

I'm going to apply the "Pirate Metrics" funnel to some important marketing and product metrics in the following two sections.

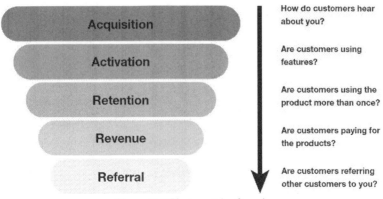

Figure 12.3 Pirate metrics funnel.

Marketing Metrics

In Chapter 10, I talked about how you may pursue a number of channels depending on where your customer is hanging out.

You might have content marketing for search, social media to generate leads, and email marketing campaigns to engage customers periodically.

You ultimately want to know which marketing channel is effective, and to figure that out we're going to apply McClure's "Pirate Metrics" funnel.

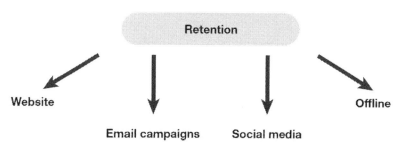

Figure 12.4 Various marketing channels you need to track metrics for.

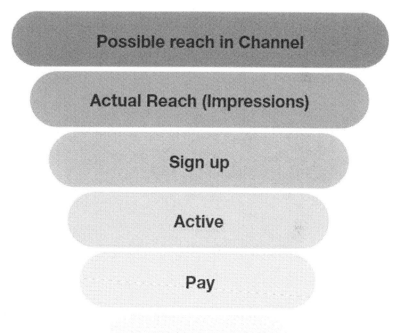

Figure 12.5 You'll want to keep track of the funnel for each channel.

Product Metrics

Similar to marketing metrics, there is also a funnel for product metrics.

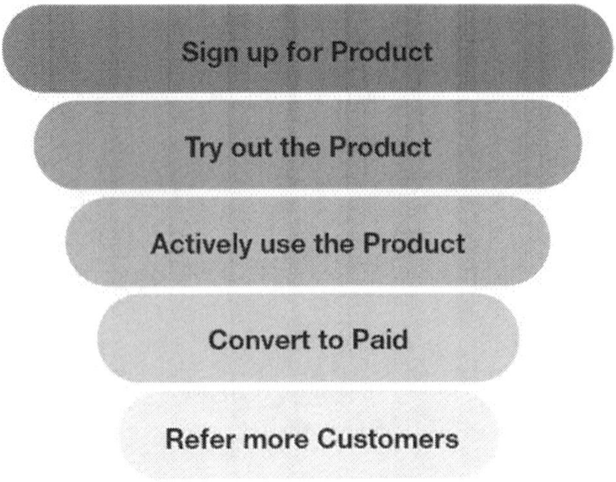

Figure 12.6 Product metrics funnel.

Before you build out your funnel you need to understand the type of product you are creating and its usage.

Are you creating a SaaS (software as a service) application with a specific purpose, such as Dropbox[65] or HelloSign[66] where the frequency of usage depends on the type of customer?

Do you expect your product to be used daily like Facebook, Google, and Twitter?

Or is it a product that is based on less-frequent customer behaviors, such AirBnB[67] and Mobissimo?[68] In the case of AirBnB, they don't expect customers to book a place to stay every day, unless they are really itinerant! With Mobissimo, customers don't do travel-based searches more than once a month.

Ultimately, product metrics boil down to measuring engagement, which in turn impacts product adoption and pricing.

For example, if you know your product will only be used once, then you can't wait for 6 months to monetize customers! You have to act quickly and create a powerful first-time experience.

Also consider which features will create triggers to monetization, and think about how you can design an experience that will set off those triggers.

If you want to know if users are actually using those features or how they are utilizing your product, I'd highly recommend using a tool like Kissmetrics[69] or Mixpanel[70].

These will keep track of how your customers flow through your product. You'll also be able to spot sections that your customers don't use. You can use this data to decide how you want to re-design workflows and attract users to particular features.

Customer Metrics

When it comes to customer metrics, our end goal is to figure out what keeps customers happy and buying! The ultimate goal is to generate repeat sales, and that can be accomplished through retaining customers and having happy customers send you referrals.

Below are some popular customer metrics, along with when it makes sense to track them:

- **Number of customers:** This can sometimes be a vanity metric, so you'll want to make sure you're keeping track of the growth rate either week by week or month by month.

- **Recency:** If you're in a business like Mobissimo then you'll want to know when you last saw a customer. If it was pretty recently then chances are it might be a while before you can monetize them again.

- **Retention rate:** If you're running a subscription-based business or put people on some form of contract, then you'll need to keep track of how many customers you retain each month. If the retention rate is high, that is a leading indicator that your product and business are appealing to your customers and that they find long-term value in it.

- **Churn rate:** This is the opposite of retention. It's basically the cancellation rate of your product if it's a monthly subscription or contract based. If you're selling a product that people pay for just once, then you'll want to track chargebacks (i.e., how often customers call their credit card company to contest a charge because they're unhappy) and refund rates (i.e., how many return the product).

- **Lifetime value:** Take a snapshot of all your customers in aggregate, calculate how much they each paid you in total, and then look at the median of all your customers' lifetime values.

- **Customer acquisition cost:** You'll want to track the sales and marketing channel each customer came from and then divide that by how much you spent on that channel in total to acquire them.

- **Customer profitability:** This basically boils down to subtracting LTV of a customer from how much you are spending on them on average. This includes things like customer services and support.

- **Net Promoter Score:** This is the percentage of people who will go on to promote your product minus the number of detractors—people who won't promote it. Currently, the best way to get this number is to survey existing and past customers.

In addition to these metrics, you'll also want to keep track of:

- **Prospects:** people who are interested but have yet to purchase.

- **First-time buyers:** people who have only purchased once.

- **Early repeat buyers:** people who have purchased more than once.

- **Core customers:** people who repeatedly purchase from you and might also refer more customers your way.

- **Core defectors:** people who churn out.

This will feed into a nice customer funnel much like the product and marketing funnels, and you'll have a sense of how many prospects you need to talk to and what it takes for them to eventually become core customers.

Keeping track of customer metrics lets us do three things:

1. **Reward** those who are loyal and profitable by creating incentives for them.

2. **Grow** by focusing marketing efforts on attracting customers who are loyal and profitable.

3. **Fire** those who aren't profitable. Not every customer is a fit, and you'll want to be sure that you're clear in your messaging. If you try to attract customers who aren't a fit, then they won't have a worthwhile experience and you won't benefit from positive word-of-mouth marketing.

Pricing Metrics

In Chapter 11 we talked about how to price. When it comes to price, there are really 3 core metrics: volume, margins, and reservation price.

I've already introduced reservation price, but I want to emphasize that the reservation price may change over time. The reservation price changes for a number of reasons: you may go after a different customer, you might decide to add more value to the product, or you may strip things away. It will also change if additional competitors come into the market.

When it comes to volume-based pricing, you'll want to understand whether that is indeed something your customers will find value in. If you decide to go the route of offering a metered pricing model, it also needs to be aligned with the user's persona. For example, I know MailChimp does this particularly well by understanding the cross section of how much money people are willing to pay to send out X number of emails. Their assumption is that the more emails you send out then the more you can probably afford to send out. They also want to get people hooked on their product, so they start by offering a new customer 2,000 emails for free. The assumption is that by the time you hit 2,001 emails, you're probably growing and can afford to spend $30-$50/month.

Finally, if you're using a distribution channel like a mobile store, know that you'll need to give them a cut for each download. You'll need to factor that margin[71] in to how much you want to charge for the product in order to make a profit.

One Metric That Matters

In the book *Lean Analytics*, the authors, Alistair Croll and Ben Yoskovitz, go into great detail of the types of metrics each type of software product and business model should keep track of. However, they know that this can be a lot for a team to manage and tie back to 1-2 business goals. Hence, they conclude by talking about the *One Metric That Matters*. The metric is primarily based on your current stage of business.

For example, right now you might just care about customers coming to your site and signing up. Later on, you might care about converting from free to paid. And once your business is quite sizable, you might care about customer profitability.

The metric that you set should guide the activities that you and your team are pursuing. If you care about customers coming to your site and signing up, then there is no point in ironing out all the minute details of a particular feature. Instead, you want to concentrate on the activities that are going to get people to sign up for your product—in this case, it translates to lots of marketing!

Similarly, if reducing churn rate becomes the one metric that matters, then you'll want to understand what it is about the customer's experience with the product or company that is causing them to cancel, then fix those issues. You don't necessarily want to make attracting brand-new customers a top priority at this time, because it's highly likely they will also churn out.

Exercise 12.1: Set one goal for your product.

I want you to set a goal, define one metric that goes along with it, and list the activities you think you should pursue to accomplish that goal.

Exercise 12.2: Set up Google Analytics.[72]

Objective: Keep track of traffic coming to your site.

Directions:

The tool you're using to create your landing pages might already include analytics. However, I still like to suggest using Google Analytics for a couple reasons. First, if you wind up hiring a marketer they are going to be more familiar with Google Analytics than any particular landing page tool. Second, a lot of tools actually pull their data from Google Analytics but don't have as rich of a data set as Google's.

A couple of things you should keep in mind: Google Analytics will only provide traffic data for days that have passed and pages that are public. If you have a page that is behind a login, Google

Analytics cannot penetrate it. See the Google Analytics website[73] for instructions on how to install the Google Analytics tracking code on your website.

Once you've set up Google Analytics, it will take about 24 hours for it to generate data.

Exercise 12.3: Add metrics to the roadmap.

Objective: Create a hypothesis about the baseline metrics you'd like to see for each feature you're building in your product roadmap.

Directions:

1. Pull out your product roadmap from Chapter 9 Exercise 9.1.

2. Create a metric for each feature (e.g., 100 signups, a 1% conversion rate from free to paying customers, or $100/day in revenue).

3. After shipping the features, revisit the metric goals you set to see if you were able to hit them.

In doing this exercise over time, you'll start to understand whether you are setting realistic or unrealistic metric goals for each feature.

Review

To gauge whether all our efforts are paying off, we want to keep track of some metrics. Metrics measure the performance of a product or business. Analytics is the discovery of meaningful patterns you spot in the data that help you make decisions.

We've covered a number of types of metrics: marketing, product, customer, and pricing. While each of these are important, you'll want to arrive at *"One Metric That Matters,"* which depends on the stage of your business.

Ultimately, we track metrics to help us make decisions, and those decisions should in turn drive the activities that people on your team pursue. Know that metrics will change as your product and business changes, but they should be always be driven by 1-2 high-level business goals.

Interview with Thomson Nguyen, CEO and Co-founder of Framed Data

Framed Data[74] takes data from businesses and turns it into actionable insights and decisions. They train, optimize, and store production date models in the cloud and provide predictions through an API, eliminating infrastructure overhead. They also provide dashboards and scenario analysis tools that tell you which company levers are driving metrics you care about.[75]

When building a new product, many people explore an industry outside of their primary expertise. However, there is something to be said for leveraging one's experience, which is what Thomson Nguyen has done. As you read through the interview with Thomson, you'll see how each experience he had gave him a deeper understanding of data science. He eventually went on to start Framed Data with his co-founder and college friend Elliott Block. You'll also learn the importance of talking to customers before writing code!

Poornima: "Hi Thomson! Thanks again for agreeing to do this interview with me."

Thomson: "You're welcome."

Poornima: "Let's start with your background. What was your major in college?"

Thomson: "I come from a family of engineers, and I am the only non-engineer. I majored in mathematics and minored in English at Berkeley. So, pretty much the black sheep of the family. My parents thought I'd go on to teach."

Poornima: "Haha, yeah, I can relate. I come from a family of engineers too, and wanted to be a lawyer for the longest time. But tech was just in my blood. So when did you learn to program?"

Thomson: "My senior year I joined a computer lab at Berkeley and had tasks similar to being a sysadmin. Then I went to grad school to study computational biology, and that's when I was introduced to coding for a living. Then I spent a year at NYU working on machine learning with Bud Mishra—that's when I was introduced to data science."

Poornima: "What got you to move back to the West Coast?"

Thomson: "I was debating between pursuing a career in banking or consulting, but then decided to move back to California in 2011. I joined Lookout, which makes security products for mobile phones. I worked as a data scientist applying my machine learning background to detecting mobile malware. After that I joined Causes, where I was reunited with my friend from college, Elliot Block. We were working on data warehousing and data engineering, basically working on processing large amounts of data."

Poornima: "So what inspired you to eventually start Framed Data?"

Thomson: "In July of 2013 I had an idea for a company. I realized that people don't care about the methodology behind the data; they just want the output. And the output they really care about is retention and conversions (getting customers to go from free to paid)."

Poornima: "Who was your initial customer segment?"

Thomson: "We targeted product managers and marketers, and made it dead simple for them to track retention, which meant they didn't need to write or cut and paste any code."

Poornima: "What did you do after you nailed down the customer segment?"

Thomson: "We applied to Y Combinator and were in the Spring 2014 batch. We've just finished it and we're serving about 600 companies."

Poornima: "What is your growth strategy going forward?"

Thomson: "We're focusing on creating an ecosystem for learning. Basically, teaching people what causes churn in their products and how they can retain customers. This lets us be less salesy, focus more on content, and generate inbound interest."

Poornima: "Now, I know that a lot of the people who are building software products care about the top of the funnel and customer acquisition. How do you get them to focus on retention and churn?"

Thomson: "Yes, you're right, most companies are focused on customer acquisition, but they need to retain them. It's the only way to create a prosperous business, so we focus on messaging that to customers. Our product makes it easy to predict on a very granular level whether someone is going to upgrade or cancel. For example, we can show how likely someone is to make an in-app purchase, and then people can take that information and market to those customers. So we're probably more of a marketing automation product rather than a data analytics product."

Poornima: "Let's switch gears and talk about your initial product. What was in the MVP?"

Thomson: "We built a really simple MVP using Python and Twitter Bootstrap with R scripts running in the background. We shipped it as fast as we could build. It broke a lot initially."

Poornima: "That's a really important step! I think people worry too much about perfecting the prototype rather than getting it out there and into the hands of customers."

Thomson: "Yeah, once we got it up it was easier to get validation. We've since re-written it in Clojure with Clojure scripts so it's more robust, and we use Om on the front-end."

Poornima: "What has been the hardest part?"

Thomson: "We struggled initially cycling through ideas, thinking about consumer applications. But then we decided to stick to our strengths in data science and machine learning."

Poornima: "I think it's great that you kept that focus. It's still a pretty young field and you've got the expertise in it. Any concluding takeaways for engineers or technical folks out there who are thinking about transitioning to being an entrepreneur?"

Thomson: "Take the leap and declare you're going to start, not that you'll do it someday. It's a different mindset, because when you decide then you ask yourself, 'What's the next step? Ok, I have to fill out some paperwork and look for an idea.' Then just break it down day by day. I was biased to start coding, but the heart of business is to sell something. You have to figure out what customers want and will use. Too many people focus on building their solutions. Instead, focus on the problem—it saves time coding."

Poornima: "Those are great takeaways, Thomson. I'm always encouraging students to talk to customers first, then build once they get validation. Great to see that you've applied the same strategy. Thank you for the interview and I wish you and Framed Data much success!"

Just to recap, here's what we learned from Thomson Nguyen:

1. **You can apply your expertise and stick to your strengths when building a product.** Thomson had ideas for other products, but decided to focus on building a product around his core expertise, data science and machine learning.

2. **You can ship a prototype that is very simple.** Once you do, it's easier to get validation. Don't focus on making it perfect before you put it out there, because you can always go back and rebuild.

3. **You want to focus on discovering a customer's problem rather than your particular idea or solution.** This will save you time when building.

Chapter 13

Successful Launch Strategies

I've contributed to more than a handful of launches. Probably the most successful and public one to date has been Mint.com's launch at the original TechCrunch40 competition, where we walked away as winners of a nice $50K check! It was definitely an atypical launch.

I've learned from both successful and underwhelming launches that you get more than one chance. While launch day is important, it's not what is going to make or break your product's success. A very successful launch can set a good tone, but you can't become complacent. I've come across too many products that had awesome launch days, only to see them fizzle out shortly thereafter. I've also experienced launches where I heard crickets; although they felt like catastrophic failures, it was possible to rebound quickly.

So, while this chapter is going to set you up for success, know that launch day isn't everything unless you're building software for SpaceX.

By now you're probably eager to get your product out the door and into the hands of customers. Or, maybe you're a little bit apprehensive because you're worried that it's just not perfect. Perhaps you've already launched but are only hearing crickets. Well, don't worry. In this chapter I'm going to cover a number of strategies to give your product a successful launch.

Section 1

Pre-launch prep

There are 3 S's to a successful launch: security, scale, and support. Up until now I haven't pushed infrastructure requirements for your product, but I will highly recommend setting up some security and compliance measures so you launch with the 3 S's ready to go. I've listed the most basic below:

1. **Encrypt usernames and passwords.** As simple as this sounds, the last thing you want is for a security breach to impact your launch day.

2. **Set up an SSL certificate for your website.** This means that your site will start with **https://** rather than **http://**. If you just have a public-facing website with no login, then it's OK to not have an SSL certificate. But if you have created a login-based website, then you definitely need to have an SSL certificate. Otherwise, your users will be susceptible to various forms of snooping and attacks. You can read up on SSL certificates[76] on Wikipedia.

3. **Set up a data backup mechanism.** Depending on who is hosting your product, they might already do hourly or daily backups. But it's always good to check.

4. **Secure log files.** If you are writing things out to a log, those must also be clear of cleartext passwords and logins.

5. **Expire sessions (unless requested).** I know a lot of people want to keep their sessions alive indefinitely. You can offer this service if you'd like, but keep in mind that you may want to monitor devices and IP addresses to make sure that someone's account isn't being hijacked.

6. **Be transparent about cookies.** If you absolutely need to store cookies, ask permission to store them and make sure it's clear to your customers why you're doing it. Read TRUSTe's blog post[77] on the best practices for doing this.

7. **PCI Compliance.** If you plan to take any form of payment, then I recommend integrating with a third-party vendor like Stripe[78] or BalancedPayments[79].

8. **Spam Act.** If your product sends out emails to customers or on behalf of customers, check out the Can Spam Act, and make sure you're compliant.[80]

This is just the tip of the iceberg when it comes to security and compliance measures, which I believe are just as important as building a product. You might decide to throw caution to the wind, but there are a lot of people trolling the Internet looking to hack young products. If you're unaware of the security measures mentioned above, then I highly recommend doing more research on them. Some companies that offer a lot of great literature and tools are TRUSTe[81] and Verisign[82].

Next, you'll want to test the product internally, giving it to a handful of trustworthy early adopters and putting some mechanisms in place to track usage and collect feedback.

Remember back to the chapter on Metrics that Matter? This is when you want to take the time to install an analytics tool like Kissmetrics or Mixpanel into your product so that you can track usage.

We always plan for the downside, but what about the upside? Can your product handle 100 concurrent customers? What about 1,000 or 10,000? If you're not sure whether your product can scale, then you'll want to do some load testing. Check out loader.io[83] or LoadImpact[84].

You'll also want to test it across various popular browsers. Check out BrowserStack[85] to help automate browser testing.

Next you'll want to set up a few customer support and application monitoring tools:

- A landing site, which is the public facing site where customers are going to come and sign up to try out your product, but they are also coming here to look for things like an About page, a Contact page, FAQs, testimonials, and video tutorials. Keep in mind that this web presence will grow alongside your product.

- A live chat client like Olark[86] to be able to message customers as they come to your website. You'll place this on your landing site.

- A ticketing tool for customers to report bugs and any issues they experience, like GetSatisfaction[87], HelpScout[88], UserVoice[89], or ZenDesk[90].

- Graceful error handling so your customers won't get pissed off if they cannot log in. Check out Status Pages[91].

- A performance monitoring tool like New Relic[92], because you'll want to know if any bottlenecks emerge once you start to put some load on your product.

Section 2

Priming your customers

Whenever people tell me they heard crickets on launch day, I ask them what their launch sequence was, and of course, they look bewildered.

A launch sequence is a set of marketing campaigns you send out to prime your initial set of customers. Yes, you have to prime them!

If you just send out an email the day of launch, don't expect people to just drop everything they are doing and try out your product.

You'll want to send out a sequence of emails to your network, early adopters, and whoever signed up to try out your product. You want to do this at least a month in advance. Ideally, you'll send out about 4-5 reminders. You might feel like you're being spammy but people need constant reminders.

On launch day before you flip the switch to go live, you'll want to send out one final reminder.

You're not quite done once the product is live. The day after, you want to reach out to customers and ask how things went. Following up is the key to getting feedback!

If you are eager to line up press and influencers to help you spread the word on launch day, then I highly recommend reaching out to them at least 2 months in advance and keeping them primed with a few reminders along the way. I recently came across Press Friendly[93], a service that lets you pitch your product to various press outlets and includes a press advisor to help with the process.

Depending on how launch day goes, you'll want to let things simmer for a couple days—maybe even a week—because at this stage the feedback won't be settling. It may all be really positive or really negative. After a while, sit down with the feedback and segment it. Know that you cannot fix everything at once, and not everything needs to be fixed or refined immediately! Software evolves slowly.

Exercise 13.1: Create a 90-day launch plan.

Objective: Develop an awareness of all the non-product tasks you need to complete in order to have a successful launch.

Directions:

Start with a high-level breakdown of what needs to get done. Here is a start:

- Contact press and pitch stories
- Create a landing site with FAQs, How-Tos, and a pricing page

---

- Send out an initial email about the launch and schedule the rest of the emails in the campaign to go out periodically

- Set up payment forms

- Set up security measures

- Set up analytics tools

- Perform internal testing

- Perform load testing

- Set up customer support channels and feedback tools

As you create your plan, you'll want to assign areas of ownership to your team and drill into the details to expose scope creep. Finally, decide if 90 days is a realistic timeframe from where you are today. If it's really tight, is there anything you can cut that will still convey the value proposition of what you have to offer?

The goal of this launch isn't to deliver something perfect, but to put something out there so that you can get some feedback. The longer you wait and continue to build, the longer it takes to truly validate your idea.

Section 3

Iterations

One of my favorite flavors of ice cream is Ben & Jerry's "Half Baked." I just love the gooey brownie batter and chunks of cookie dough. In fact, I love it more than when people serve a fully-baked brownie or cookie a la mode.

Software is like Ben & Jerry's "Half Baked" ice cream. It's never quite done, and that's what makes it delicious! Unlike hardware or a physical product, you can iterate on it constantly, but the key is to pick a just couple things to improve—not everything.

You'll want to sit down and sift through feedback from all your channels: customer support tickets, calls, chats, and emails. Keep track of outliers, like feedback that was extremely positive and extremely negative. You'll want to reach out to these folks. The extremely positive ones will become great case studies. Those who are negative may have valid concerns, depending on how constructive they are. Finally, look for the common criticisms.

You'll want to marry this anecdotal feedback with data; your tool to track analytics (such as KISSmetrics or Mixpanel) will be helpful here. You'll be able to see exactly what your customers did and did not explore. This will help you decide where you want to focus your efforts going forward. I cannot tell you how many times I've heard of people refining the wrong workflows or features only to find out later that no one was using them! If you want to use your time wisely, set up a tool that tracks customer paths and provides you with analytics so you know which ones to work on.

At this stage, the name of the game is iterate. But once again, you have to go back to setting up some hypotheses.

Section 4

Pinpointing problem areas

To identify problem areas, you have to revisit your metrics to figure out where you want to focus. Then, create hypotheses about why the metric is lower or higher than desired and test some solutions.

If you're not getting enough traffic to the site, you need to step up your marketing game and find more channels to spread the word about your product.

If the problem is that people are visiting the site but you're dissatisfied with the percentage of people signing up, you need to work on messaging to convince them to sign up.

If people are visiting and signing up but not paying or coming back, then you've got to focus on the product engagement. This may mean redesigning user flows, especially the first-time experience, and making it really easy for users to onboard themselves.

Section 5

Pitfalls of pivoting

Whenever things aren't going as well as you had hoped, you may experience an overwhelming desire to pivot.

However, you have to be careful about changing directions. If there are clear signs based on customer behavior and feedback, then a radical change might be necessary. But too many pivots can actually burn your team out and threaten their creativity and motivation. So before you do decide to pivot, take the time to see if people are on board—including yourself!

If you decide to go down this path, you'll want to reevaluate your product roadmap and metrics.

Types of pivots to consider:[94]

- **Zoom-in:** What was previously just a feature becomes the focus on the entire product.

- **Zoom-out:** If one feature doesn't sufficiently meet the needs of customers then it becomes part of a bigger product.

- **Customer segment:** The product might not meet the needs of the original set of customers and you need to reposition it to attract a new segment.

- **Customer need:** What you might have thought was a problem or need cannot be monetized, or you discover that there is a bigger need.

- **Platform:** The original product becomes part of a suite of products or can be leveraged for other companies to build products on.

- **Business architecture:** You may go from high margins and low volume to low margins and high volume, or vice versa.

- **Channel:** You might change how you distribute your product, which also requires repositioning it.

- **Technology:** You might decide to change the technology you are using to deliver a solution.

Section 6

Sunsetting your product

Up until this point I've been pretty positive, pushing you to validate your idea, launch, collect feedback, and iterate. However, I want to switch gears and also set your expectations. There may come a time where you discover that things just aren't working out and you might want to end-of-life your product.

A couple years ago I had to do this with the second product we launched at BizeeBee, BizeeBee Billing. We had spent nearly a year and $100K building it. While the initial launch was successful, over time, the number of issues it possessed had become more than my lean team could handle. At the end of 2012 we decided to shut it down and focus our efforts on our main membership product.

In hindsight, I'm happy I went through the effort of building the product, because it was well received. But I also learned that building and maintaining two products can be really taxing on a lean team.

The early warning signs of a product near the end of its life include consistently negative customer feedback, third-party vendor changes that cause your product to become obsolete, lack of revenue, and requirements of additional investment of time and capital that you don't currently possess.

If you decide to sunset your product, you basically have to follow the launch sequence in reverse.

You might be asking, *"You mean I cannot just shut it down and walk away?"*

Well, technically you can, but I don't recommend it if you care at all about your personal brand.

People are OK with hearing that you tried and failed, but they aren't cool with you just fleeing.

Section 7

Un-launch sequence

You want to start by motivating your team because no one likes to kill a product they painstakingly built. Then, figure out whether you can put it in a low-cost maintenance mode or if you have to turn it off completely. If you have another product in your portfolio or another company's product that you regard highly, recommend it to people as a substitute. Finally, provide reasons you are shutting down the product to your customers, give them 3-12 months of notice (not 1 day), and be prepared to off-board them.

Some customers may be pissed, but the vast majority will understand and be supportive. Even after we shut down BizeeBee Billing, a number of our customers stuck around and are still with us today.

 ## Review

Here's a quick recap. Launching is just one step, but if you want to start off on strong footing, you'll want to focus on 3 key areas: security, scale, and support. Use the 90-day Launch Plan to guide all the non-product related tasks that you need to complete. It might take you more or less time to complete each of those tasks, and that's OK.

Once you've launched, you have to take the feedback from customers, sift through it, and begin to refine the product further. As you receive feedback and refine, you may decide to pivot. If you do, you'll want to make sure your team is aligned and that you have a clear hypothesis to guide the pivot.

Finally, there may come a time where you have to shut down a product. It isn't the end of the world, and it can lead to a positive outcome if done properly.

Interview with Alyssa Ravasio, CEO and Founder of Hipcamp

Hipcamp[95] empowers people to discover, book, and share amazing campsites. With a trend of increasing urbanization, they help people get out of the city and into nature.

They make discovering a great campsite based on your dates, activities, and specific needs very easy. They do this by integrating with third parties to aggregate real-time availability information and create original content that their users need and love. So, for example, they can help you find a campsite by the ocean where you can bring your dog next weekend!

They are their own customers. They've grown up camping in California and know every nook and cranny of space—its quirks, its problems, and its enormous opportunities for improvement. They know how important it is to get out of the city and into the many parks they have at their doorsteps. They live and breathe camping and know more about this problem than anyone else.[96]

Alyssa Ravasio was a scholarship student in my Lean Product Development Course. I chose to interview her for this book because I wanted to showcase someone who didn't start off as an engineer or developer but learned how to code in order to build a product on her own.

As you read through the interview, you'll learn how Alyssa has managed to stay scrappy and successfully build Hipcamp.

Poornima: "Hi Alyssa! Thanks for taking the time to do an interview with me today. It's great to see how much Hipcamp has grown since you started working on it in my course a year ago. But before we dig into Hipcamp, let's start off with your background. How did you get interested in tech?"

Alyssa: "I initially majored in film at UCLA. Then I participated in a class called 'Engineers & Poets' about how the Internet was going to change our world: our economies and how we socialize. I then decided to design my own major, and it was called Digital Democracy. I learned some HTML and CSS and had built static websites, but I didn't learn how to code in college."

Poornima: "What did you do after you graduated?"

Alyssa: "I did an internship with the State Department, then went to work at a startup called Revel Systems. They were building an iPad POS [point of sale] system."

Poornima: "And what was your role at Revel?"

Alyssa: "I did sales, customer support, and product management. I'd talk to all the current and potential customers, then prioritize feedback. Then I realized that I wanted to learn how to program to bring my ideas to reality."

Poornima: "What was your process for learning how to code?"

Alyssa: "I learned about DevBootcamp from a friend at a party. I just showed up when they were starting the next class. The people who were running it liked my moxie but told me I had to wait for the next class. So I did, and then I went through the program."

Poornima: "What did you do after you graduated?"

Alyssa: "I asked myself, *'Do I know enough to build out a prototype?'* And I got a scholarship to attend your Lean Product Development Course. Had that not happened, I probably would have just taken a job."

Poornima: "Wow, that is wonderful to hear! But what really convinced you that it was the right time and idea?"

Alyssa: "I met Steve Huffman, the founder of Hipmunk and Reddit, around that time. Steve convinced me that I shouldn't look back and just do it. So I began building the prototype during your course."

Poornima: "And what happened after you launched the prototype?"

Alyssa: "I sent it out to 40 people. 1 person who responded said that he was looking to build a similar product. His name is Eric Bach, and he is now my co-founder."

Poornima: "That's awesome! Who was your first customer?"

Alyssa: "We got California State Park in Sonoma to use it."

Poornima: "Great to see that you were able to validate the prototype with a customer."

Alyssa: "Yeah, it was good to put it out there. Next, I experimented and found out that people would be willing to pay to book a campsite online. But I also realized that I needed a more robust site. So I ended up rebuilding it in Rails and launching it in February 2014."

Poornima: "How have you been funding the development?"

Alyssa: "I had some personal savings."

Poornima: "Kudos to you for staying scrappy for the past year! I know you've recently been talking to an angel investor. How did that come about?"

Alyssa: "Dave Morin, who is an angel investor, found my site and reached out to me."

Poornima: "It does pay to put something out there! OK, I want to switch gears and talk specifically about how you came up with the idea for Hipcamp."

Alyssa: "I'm a very outdoorsy person. I love nature. So back in 2013 I was looking for a campsite for New Year's. I went online and had a horrible time. There were national versus state versus county parks, and it was all disorganized. I spent hours looking for a campsite. I finally found one. When I arrived at the campsite, I realized that it was on the beach, and I hadn't brought my surfboard to enjoy it! That's when I realized the system is really broken."

Poornima: "You pursued an idea based on a passion you had for the outdoors! OK, any final takeaways for our readers who might be mulling over an idea or the decision to build a product?"

Alyssa: "The only thing that limits what you're capable of is what you believe you can do. Learn how to code only if you want to code. But do not if you just want to build a company. In that case, it's better to find others to build it for you. Finally, you should be obsessed with the problem, not your solution. You want to solve a problem and make an impact that leaves you feeling proud of yourself."

Poornima: "Those are fantastic, Alyssa! Thanks again for taking the time to share your journey. I wish you and Hipcamp continued success."

Just to recap, here's what we learned from Alyssa Ravasio:

1. **Put your prototype out there.** In Alyssa's case, doing so led to getting her first customer and finding her co-founder.

2. **You can rebuild your prototype to be more robust.** Alyssa rebuilt her prototype after she received feedback from her first customer and validated that people would pay to book a campsite.

3. **Learn to code if you want to know how to code, otherwise find someone to build a prototype for you.** In Alyssa's case, she really wanted to know how to code and was considering taking a job, but then decided to build a product based on an idea she had.

4. **Be obsessed with the problem rather than the solution.** Remember, your idea is going to change, so you don't want to get too stuck on your solution; instead, focus on making a positive impact.

Chapter 14

Getting Working Capital to Build Your Product and Your Business

You may be wondering why I've included a chapter on financing in a book on building software products. As the old adage goes, "It takes money to make money." If your goal is just to build a nice product for yourself then you can skip this chapter completely. However, if your goal is to eventually build a business, then you'll need to realize that this requires capital, and I want you to have a sense of how you can get this funding. I also think there are a lot of myths about how software products are built, and I want to present you with a number of financing options so that you can choose a realistic path forward.

In this chapter I'm going to outline some ways to think about funding product development and, eventually, your business. Before we dig into each strategy, here are some definitions of all the terms I'm going to use:

- **Bootstrapping** is building a business without funding from investors.

- **Crowdfunding** is taking capital from a group of people.

- **Angel investment** is capital that you receive from a business angel or high-net-worth individual in exchange for an equity stake in your company.

- **Venture capital** is similar to angel investment in that you exchange equity (a percentage of ownership in your company) for capital. It is usually provided to companies pursuing high growth with exits like large acquisitions or IPOs. The source of the funds is typically large institutions like corporations, endowments, and trusts.

Just like people rush into building a product too quickly, I've seen people rush into fundraising. The result is that either they raise a lot of money and burn it quickly in a number of experiments, or they waste many months getting rejected from investors rather than building a real business.

Also, realize that there is a level of control that you have over an idea when you are self-funding. Once you take **OPM** (other people's money), especially from professional investors, you are expected to do things like send them frequent updates on your progress, attend meetings, and solicit their advice. This can be beneficial once you know where you're headed, but doing it prematurely will just pull you in directions that you may not like.

While it might seem like seeking outside investment is a guaranteed path to success, it isn't. There have been startups that took $1M or even $40M and ended up just closing up shop. At the same time, other startups that hadn't raised even $1 went on to build $100M+ businesses and even had IPOs!

Ultimately, it comes down to knowing the vision that you want to bring to life and which sources of capital can make it happen.

Section 1

Initial investment

The product validation steps I've listed in chapters 1 through 6 will require less than $500 of startup capital.

Once you've gone through these steps and are ready to build, I advise you to try generating revenue immediately. Create a concierge MVP if you can, or a very simple prototype if you can't, and couple it with a pre-order campaign.

I realize that you might be on the fence about doing a pre-order campaign or asking customers for money before you've built something. However, realize that making money from day one can be extremely motivating for yourself and your team. There is also a level of accountability that both you and your customers experience. The longer you put this off, the harder it becomes to understand the true value you are generating for your customers.

Section 2

How much capital do you need?

Word on the street is that software is a high-margin business, and it's gotten relatively inexpensive to build a product. This is due to several things: managed hosting that drives down server costs, the advent of frameworks in languages like Ruby and JavaScript that make creating a prototype quick and easy, and the ability to outsource development to other countries. It also doesn't cost much to acquire an initial set of customers. There are a number of low-cost options for marketing, like the ones I've highlighted in Chapter 10.

But for some reason, people forget that there are other costs associated with running a business, including overhead, employees, and legal expenses (incorporating, creating and reviewing contracts). You can put these expenses off for a while, but if you decide to grow you'll need to hire people to help you scale. While there are a number of low-cost channels to acquire a customer, you will need capital to experiment and find out which channels work for you. As you acquire customers, there will be a level of customer service you need to provide. Initially you can handle all their requests, but as you grow, you'll need help.

The biggest cost in building software is still human capital. You can start and stay scrappy by building the initial landing pages yourself. If you're technical, you can even build the prototype yourself; if you're not then you can outsource its development.

If your goal is to create a lifestyle business or have a passive source of income, then I'd recommend building a fairly simple product that doesn't require too much maintenance.

However, if your goal is to grow and scale, you will eventually need to pay a team to help with the various aspects of the business: engineering, product development, sales, marketing, and customer support.

In the chapter on product management I talked about setting realistic milestones for product development. The same is true for revenue. You want to sit down and figure out how much it's going to cost you to build your initial prototype, acquire your first set of customers, and service them!

Section 3

Begin with bootstrapping

Both Mint.com and BizeeBee were initially funded using personal savings. Aaron Patzer invested $50K of his personal savings to build out the prototype before reaching out to angel investors. I spent roughly the same when building BizeeBee's prototype. However, several of the interviews in this book highlight stories of founders who invested significantly less than that, so know that it is possible!

After building the prototype and generating revenue, I did take in some angel investment, but I went back to bootstrapping after a couple years.

When I started on the path to bootstrapping, I had little to no guidance. Most people I talked with who had bootstrapped had really just done it through savings or as a bridge before they received investment; there were very few who bootstrapped all the way to break-even and profitability.

Before we get into the nuts and bolts of bootstrapping, there is one concern I want to address: the feeling that you're not innovating because you're focused exclusively on revenue. I'm going to call a spade a spade and say that yes, it's natural to have this feeling, and it's OK. However, you've got to learn to put on the blinders.

The major benefit to bootstrapping is that it will give you the financial freedom and control that allows you to direct your company and innovate. The key to getting that freedom is to hit the revenue milestones that will let you switch from purely pursuing sales to doing creative work. I'll talk about how to think about those milestones and how to hit them in an upcoming exercise.

Section 4

Basics of bootstrapping

The 3 most common ways to bootstrap while still scaling your business are:

1. **Build a simple version of a product**, then switch your focus to customer acquisition. If this is the approach you take, then you'll want to make sure the initial version of the product has the following:

    -   A simple way for customers to onboard themselves that gives them a positive first-time experience and provides enough value that they are willing to pay (this will keep churn low).
    -   Marketing baked right into the product for increased viral distribution.

- Enough money in the bank to support yourself while you're waiting for revenue to come in.

It might seem like this approach presupposes product-market fit. However, it can be done if you spend a bulk of time doing pre-sales by selling customers on the value proposition before the product is built. Or, if you have a product that's been out there for a while—maybe as a free product—focus on getting people to become paying customers. Offer just a little value to get them interested and using the free version, but do your best to upsell them. The latter is the approach the company Olark took, and you can read more about how they did it in my interview with one of its founders, Ben Congleton, in this book.

2. **Initially offer services that are high touch**, while automating and productizing them. In this approach, you can start by doing work for an initial set of customers—essentially, consulting. This is tantamount to a concierge MVP. While doing this, you'll need to figure out a way to automate some of the work you've been doing and productize it. You can then offer the product to your customers as a time and cost-cutting tool. When doing this, realize that you'll be cannibalizing your service-based revenue stream, but eventually you'll be able to recoup the losses because your product will appeal to a wider audience and be more scalable than your service offerings.

3. **Offer services that require a level of expertise that can only come from you**, are hard to automate or replicate to experience the same level of quality, and can be a one-to-many offering.

Freelancing and consulting are the common ways people do this. However, I advise against this because you end up trading dollars for hours, which isn't very scalable. Instead, I prefer the one-to-many model, which means servicing a number of customers at the same time.

4. The classic example of this is teaching. In this approach, you can eventually productize your curriculum, but you begin with a very high-value offering that people are willing to pay a premium for. You're going to use that premium to build up reserves and possibly fund product development.

Section 5

The path I chose

My current approach is #3. I teach a course on Lean Product Development and split the proceeds between funding product development for BizeeBee and the cost of running and marketing the course. I also pursue other activities, such as speaking, that I get paid for while simultaneously building awareness and funneling customers back into my course.

But I didn't get there overnight; it took a solid year of effort and experimentation.

When I began, I was hell-bent on creating a repeatable revenue stream. So before I began, I took a sales training course from Sandler[97]. It helped me to understand:

- how revenues are tied into sales and marketing activities;

- how to become more comfortable experimenting with various sales and marketing activities and give them ample time to yield results; and

- how to measure the success of the experiments, continue to invest time and resources into the ones that work, and stop or tweak the ones that don't.

To understand your funding needs, compare what people are willing to pay with the costs associated with customer acquisition and rendering your service.

For example, after the Sandler training, I took stock of revenue I made from teaching between August 2012 and December 2012, so I knew what people would pay. A 5-month interval was good enough for me to see a pattern, and I noticed that I was making $X per month. However, I was giving away half of the revenue to schools and venues where I was teaching.

My initial goal was to keep making $X without giving third parties a cut. I needed to figure out which sales and marketing activities would lead me to generate $X without paying half of $X.

Keep in mind that if you're starting from scratch, then you'll want to have enough money to give yourself a 6- to 9-month cushion, maybe even longer. During this time, you'll be experimenting and building up data on sales and marketing activities that attract customers, as well as learning what people are willing to pay for. If you're primarily a service-based business rather than a product-based business, you have the luxury of collecting money from day one!

Always feed the funnel

In Chapter 12 I showed you a marketing funnel. Keeping the top of that funnel filled is a must when bootstrapping, which will require some experimentation.

My goal for Q1 of 2013 was to keep making $X per month by doing all the marketing and promotion to acquire customers on my own. My marketing activities were the only things that I changed and experimented with for 3 months. I kept my service the same.

Remember: when you're running an experiment, you have to keep some things constant! I've seen people change too many variables and find themselves unable to draw clear conclusions about cause and effect.

At the end of Q1, I hit my revenue goal and decided that I wanted to double $X and make $2X in Q2. Here's what I did to achieve that.

Increase revenue while keeping costs constant

When it comes to revenue, you must remember that the marketing and promotional spend it took to get to $X is not what it will take to get to $2X. Also, when you go from $X to $2X you'll incur increased operating costs if you take an approach that increases volume of sales. I didn't want my costs to go up; I wanted to spend only $Y per month. Therefore, I didn't increase volume. Instead, I focused on finding a smaller set of customers who would pay enough to get me to $2X per month.

I chose the path of attracting fewer customers because I wasn't focused on scaling; my goal was to make $Y per month to fund product development! If your goal is to scale, then you'll have to keep a close watch on how costs go up as you increase sales volume.

Be patient

Sometimes you have to stay with the same strategy for a while.

It's easy to miss goals and think it's time to change up your strategy, but I believe that it can take a while for seeds to sprout. The Sandler sales system reinforced this point, and made me feel comfortable about my approach.

In addition to keeping track of marketing and sales activities, you want to track the time and effort they take before you see progress.

Sometimes you have to think about factors like seasonality that affect buying decisions. Also recall the concept of "buy time" from the chapter on pricing; it will take time for a prospective customer to convert to a paying customer. Buy time has 2 stages: first, the amount of time it takes the customer to go from becoming aware of your business to understanding your value proposition; second, the time it takes for them to experience enough pain to decide to use your service and pay you for it.

If you see some progress but aren't sure about the results being repeatable, stick with your strategy rather than veering off course. If you constantly veer off course then you'll get trapped in a cycle of running experiments. Patience eventually leads to progress. Of course, if you see a trend of negative results consistently, you need to investigate their causes and refine your approach.

It took me Q2 and Q3 of 2013 to make $Y per month in a way that was repeatable. Much of the time was spent pursuing a small set of activities consistently and measuring their progress. As I entered Q4, it became clear which marketing and sales activities were working and which weren't. While I continued to experiment, I made sure to devote enough time and energy to the activities that were working.

Driven by sales to driven by dreams

For a while, all I did was focus on hitting my numbers and being a sales machine. But I'm a creative person, and I knew that eventually I'd get tired of chasing deals. Plus, my motivation for building a business was to live a lifestyle where I could do what I love.

To get back to creative pursuits, I needed to let prospects come to me rather than always chase them. That's when I realized that I had to focus more on value-creation activities.

I took a weekend workshop with Racheal Cook[98] to understand how to do activities that are focused on creating value and building a community, such as nurturing referrals, offering resources that provide value to prospects, and making sure offerings are clear to customers—not just in terms of value proposition, but the experience itself.

If you're going to continue to build while bootstrapping, you'll need to think about this level of refinement.

There's obviously more to share and do, but since this guide is focused on the basics, I'll stop here and summarize what we've covered on bootstrapping:

1. Figure out your service offering and start charging people for it.

2. Start by setting a small revenue goal that is repeatable. Then, figure out marketing and sales activities along with their time intervals to yield returns.

3. For the subsequent revenue goals, figure out which activities will continue to help achieve those goals and be consistent about pursuing them. Punt or refine your approach if activities demonstrate failing or inconclusive results.

4. Watch your ratio of revenue to cost, and if need be, service a smaller set of customers at higher value.

Finally, remember that there is no shame in bootstrapping through services. While your well-funded friends are worried about valuations, you can enjoy the freedom and flexibility that comes with bootstrapping!

If you'd like more case studies of software products and companies that bootstrapped their way to profitability and even an IPO, then I highly recommend reading Sramana Mitra's book *Bootstrapping with Services*.

Exercise 14.1 Create a revenue roadmap.

Objective: Create a rough estimate for how much capital you'll need to fund the initial prototype and what it will take to hit certain revenue milestones.

Directions:

1. **List out costs.** Start by listing out all the costs you'll incur for tools such as:

   - Web hosting service like BlueHost

   - Application hosting like Heroku

   - Code repository system like Github

   - Product management tool like Pivotal Track

   - SSL Certificate

2. **List out overhead expenses.** Next, figure out overhead if you plan to hire people, such as:

   - A developer

   - A designer

   - A marketer or copywriter

3. **Set a target monthly burn rate.** You'll want to total up the amount you're going to spend on costs in steps 1 and 2, then decide if you're going to spend it in a lump sum or over time. If you spend it over a period of a few months, the monthly average is known as your **monthly burn rate.**

4. **Set a target monthly run rate.** Ask yourself how much you want to make per month—in other words, your targeted

monthly run rate. If you did Exercise 11.1 in Chapter 11 then you should have a pricing model and price point. Your monthly run rate should be your price multiplied by the number of customers you service each month.

To become a profitable business, your run rate should be higher than your burn rate. For example, if you're initially offering a monthly subscription plan with 10 paying customers a month at $10, then your monthly run rate is $100, which is a great start. However, if your goal is to get to $1000/month, then you'll either need to increase your price from $10 to $100 or figure out how to attract more customers.

Attracting more customers means doing more sales and marketing; you'll need to discover more channels and you'll want to keep track of the funnel across each channel as I described in Chapter 12. You might discover that for every 10K impressions you get 10 paying customers—that's a 0.1% conversion rate. So, if you want to get more than 10 paying customers, you'll need to attract more than 10K impressions.

If you instead decide to increase the price point, you may have to find a different customer segment willing to pay the higher price, provide additional value in the product, or be clearer about the value you are offering in the product.

Hopefully by now you're starting to see how all your activities and decisions are interweaved!

5. **Consider multiple revenue streams.** Some people set goals like $5000/month revenue in 3 months or 6 months. Sometimes you're able to hit that revenue milestone, but often it takes a while to grow. Having a single revenue stream from your product may not be enough to hit that

revenue milestone. You might want to consider offering services like consulting. If you can offer services to existing or potential customers of your product then you won't feel like you're going in a number of directions. But, you still want to be careful of how much time it's going to take to render the service and settle on a realistic number of customers you can support.

There may be customers banging on your door who want you to advance the product faster. See if they are willing to pay for additional product development, and have them write you a larger check to do that. You might decide to forgo payment for the product itself if they do. However, be cautious about building for just one customer. You want to make sure you're still building a general-purpose product that can be sold to other customers. Otherwise, your business will become beholden to just one.

6. **Create a simple spreadsheet to keep track of your income and expenses.** This will help you predict when you'll become profitable. Create one sheet for income, another for expenses, and a final one for profit.

	January 2014	February 2014	March 2014
Rent	1500	1500	1500
Employee 1	5000	5000	5000
Employee 2			
Service 1			
Service 2			
Total Monthly Expenses	6500	6500	6500

Figure 14.1 Income and expenses spreadsheet.

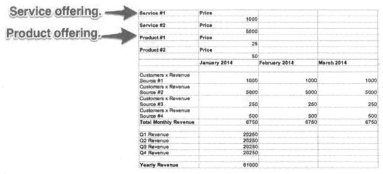

Service offering. →

Product offering. →

Service #1	Price			
		1000		
Service #2	Price			
		5000		
Product #1	Price			
		25		
Product #2	Price			
		50		
		January 2014	February 2014	March 2014
Customers x Revenue Source #1				
		1000	1000	1000
Customers x Revenue Source #2				
		5000	5000	5000
Customers x Revenue Source #3				
		250	250	250
Customers x Revenue Source #4				
		500	500	500
Total Monthly Revenue		6750	6750	6750
Q1 Revenue		20250		
Q2 Revenue		20250		
Q3 Revenue		20250		
Q4 Revenue		20250		
Yearly Revenue		81000		

Figure 14.2 Service and product offerings spreadsheet.

Yearly Expenses	78000	Total from expenses sheet.
Yearly Earnings	81000	Total from income sheet.
Yearly Gross Profits	3000	Subtract the first from the second.

Figure 14.3 Profit spreadsheet.

7. **Keep in mind that this is a very simple model.** Depending on your pricing model you'll need to factor in churn rate (i.e., the % of customers that leave each month if you're doing a monthly subscription) or % of refunds if it's a one-time purchase.

Just like how you have a product roadmap, you now have a revenue roadmap that you can use to guide your decisions when it comes to monetization and marketing activities. Even if you decide to go down the path of fundraising you can reuse this revenue roadmap because investors will ask you for financial projections, and that's exactly what it includes. You might want to add accelerators in there, like additional talent and marketing activities you may pursue based on the amount of funding you receive.

Crowdfunding

There are two types of crowdfunding. First, there is traditional crowdfunding, which is raising capital from close friends and family. Second, there is the modern version, done through platforms like Kickstarter[99] and Indiegogo[100].

Most successful crowdfunding campaigns that used Kickstarter and Indiegogo have been for consumer product goods rather than software. Platforms like Fundly[101] are product agnostic.

Before you decide to go the route of crowdfunding, be sure to check what types of products are acceptable on the platform because the rules are often in flux.

The requirements for crowdfunding are similar to doing a pre-order campaign with a landing page:

- You need to have a clear value proposition for your product.

- You'll need pricing tiers that appeal to people's needs.

- If the product is still in development then you need to set clear expectations for when the product will be available.

However, unlike a pre-order campaign where customers are primarily concerned with a product that meets their needs, crowdfunders care more about *why* you are building this product. Hence, you'll need to have a story that showcases your vision.

I also recommend figuring out how much you need to raise in order to hit your next milestone—and don't forget to factor in the transaction fee you need to pay the platform provider.

The success of a crowdfunding campaign is contingent on how much setup work you do. Here are the basics:

- You'll want to start by reaching out to your network to let them know you're doing a crowdfunding campaign. Getting the support of these folks is a great way to seed the campaign.

- When the campaign kicks off, you'll want to remind your network that it's time to fund, and this is the ideal time to ask them to help spread the word!

- Toward the end of the campaign, you want to make one final marketing push in order to hit your goal amount.

After you've raised money, you'll need to keep the people who funded you in the loop about your product's progress. If you miss a deadline, communicate the reasoning behind it; people are forgiving as long as you're upfront and honest with them!

Section 7

Accelerators

Over the past few years a number of accelerators have popped up. Some have a vertical focus like financial tech or healthcare, but most are pretty general. The goal is to help accelerate a company's growth (i.e., customer acquisition and revenues). Some others are earlier-stage, like incubators, and are focused on helping founders get products out of their heads. And finally, there are those that are really just glorified co-working spaces that may provide access to a number of resources, like technical talent and investor introductions.

If you're considering an accelerator, take the time to do some research to understand if it's right for you and for the stage you're in. There are subtle nuances to each, so be sure to understand how a particular one can help.

If you live outside of Silicon Valley or just don't have a strong network that can introduce you to angel investors, then you may consider applying to an accelerator like AngelPad[102], 500 Startups[103], TechStars[104], or Y Combinator[105].

There is no guarantee that you'll get in, and even if you do, it doesn't mean you'll definitely be able to raise capital. However, a number of these accelerators pride themselves on having a network of angels that they can introduce you to, so you stand a better chance of getting introduced to angels than if you go at it alone.

Some will also give you capital in exchange for equity. Currently, 500 Startups and Y Combinator provide about $100K to each incoming company in exchange for equity. The range is usually 3-7% ownership, but it can vary.

Most accelerators have an application process that aims to understand what stage you're in so that they know whether or not they can help you. They'll want to know the following:

- Do you have a co-founder?

- What is your team composition (i.e., the number of technical versus business people involved)?

- Have you launched yet?

- Who are you customers?

- How many do you have?

- How do you acquire them (i.e., what are your distribution channels)?

- What is your pricing model?

- Are you currently making money?

- Do you have metrics like CAC (customer acquisition cost), LTV (lifetime value of a customer), or annual run rate (how much money do you make each year)?

Their goals in asking these questions are to find out if you know your business and your market, and if you've done enough work to show that you are committed to furthering your idea.

Accelerators have varying batch sizes and run their programs periodically throughout the year. AngelPad takes in about a dozen companies twice a year (one batch in San Francisco and another in New York City), 500 Startups accepts about 30-40 companies across four batches a year (two in San Francisco and two in Mountain View, CA), and Y-Combinator takes in about 60-80 companies across two batches (all based in Mountain View, CA).

Many people also benefit from the camaraderie of being with other founders who are facing similar challenges of building their products and scaling their businesses.

Getting rejected from an accelerator isn't the end of the world and doesn't mean your idea sucks! Often it means that it's not yet time to accelerate your growth. You need to run more experiments on your own first. Some even encourage you to reapply once you're further along.

Section 8

Fundraising from investors

I'm going to provide a brief overview of fundraising from investors. Please realize there is more research to be done if you do indeed want to go the path of fundraising. I highly recommend checking out the following resources to get a deeper understanding of investment, how the investment community operates, and what they are currently:

- AVC[106] by Fred Wilson

- Ben Horowitz[107]

- Haywire[108] by Semil Shah

- Venture Hacks[109]

The landscape for fundraising is in constant flux. It used to be that having a bright idea and pitching it to the right investors could get you investment capital. While there are more angel investors today than in the past, the bar for garnering investment has gone up. Therefore, you have to be careful about how you approach the process. Don't jump right into it otherwise you'll end up wasting time that you could have spent building your product and business.

However, even after I say this, I know people try to approach investors with nothing but an idea. Unless you've previously sold your company for millions of dollars, investors will not want to risk investing in an unknown person until you have some **traction**.

Traction today means:

- at least having a prototype built out, and preferably one that is being used by paying customers; as well as

- a solid team of seasoned technical people, along with business people who are doing sales or marketing to help with customer growth.

Finally, you need to have a BIG idea, which means that it needs to expand to service a large market segment. This is often where many people get tripped up. Just having a technical product doesn't mean you have a big idea. It's OK if you are operating in a niche market if you can show how you'll expand to other market segments or how you'll grow the market.

An example of a company that has grown the market would be AirBnB. Initially, investors thought, "Who would want to rent a room from an unknown person?" Turns out it was a behavior that was already prevalent, but it was just being done in a limited social context. To do it at scale would require a few things, including building up trust and awareness, while still focusing on a market segment that enjoyed travel or hosting people in their homes. Hence, as AirBnB was building, it was also responsible for growing the market and increasing awareness.

Section 9

The difference between angels and venture capitalists

Angels are individuals who have a high net worth and are investing their own money. Venture capitalists are professional investors who raise capital from limited partners (LPs), like corporations, high-net-worth individuals, and endowments.

In the early stages you'll want to approach angels, who are willing to take a bigger risk, rather than venture capitalists, who are concerned about providing returns to their LPs.

A typical angel investment would be $10K to $1M.

An initial investment round, also known as a seed round, can range from $50K-$2M, and come from a combination of angels and VCS or either one exclusively.

As I mentioned before, if you don't have a strong network, you'll either need to take the time to cultivate one that is composed of angel investors, or you'll want to consider an accelerator program. While there are a number of services that provide a directory of angels, like AngelList,[110] there is still an element of trust and relationship building that needs to take place before someone feels comfortable enough to invest.

Section 10

When to consider venture capital

One of the reasons many entrepreneurs come out to Silicon Valley is to raise capital from venture capitalists. While tech media makes it seem like everyone here raises capital—and a lot of it—fairly easily, the reality is that it is still pretty hard to get investment from VCs.

If you are going to go the route of seeking capital from VCs, then realize you're going to need to find an investor who is interested in your market, because some (though not all) have a thesis around the types of ideas and industries they like to invest in. You'll also need to be willing to give up a larger portion of equity in your company, anywhere from 15-30%. You'll need to give them a board seat, which means that they now have a voting right when it comes to major decisions related to your company. You also need to have a plan in place for taking in and using a large amount of capital, because investors are giving you growth capital. Once again, the market is in flux, but currently most VCs want to invest a minimum of $2M-$3M.

In exchange, VCs will give you a valuation (i.e., what they think your company is worth). The valuation is tied back to the amount of capital they invest. For example, if a VC wants a 20% take in your company, they might give you a $2M investment and value your company at $10M.

Ultimately, you need to be ready to grow your business and convince the VC that your idea can scale to a large market.

Review

We've talked about 4 ways of getting funding for your product idea: bootstrapping, crowdfunding, angel investment, and venture capital investment. Each requires some amount of planning and has tradeoffs associated with it. Before you decide to go down a particular path, you need to take the time to set some milestones for your business and understand the amount of capital you need to get to those milestones. You also need to understand how the sales and marketing activities you pursue will impact your customer growth.

Interview with David Cummings, CEO and Co-founder of Pardot

Pardot[111] offers a software-as-a-service marketing automation application that allows marketing and sales departments to create, deploy, and manage online marketing campaigns that increase revenue and maximize efficiency. Pardot features certified CRM [customer relationship management] integrations with salesforce.com, NetSuite, Microsoft Dynamics CRM, and SugarCRM. It empowers marketers with lead nurturing, lead scoring, and ROI reporting to generate and qualify sales leads, shorten sales cycles, and demonstrate marketing accountability.

Pardot was founded in 2007 by David Cummings and Adam Blitzer in Atlanta, GA. The founders bootstrapped their way to over $10 million in revenue and sold to ExactTarget in 2012 for $95.5M. ExactTarget was later acquired by SalesForce in 2013 for $2.5B.

Since Pardot's acquisition, David has gone on to start Kevy[112] and Atlanta Ventures[113].

As you read my interview with David, you'll learn how he started his first business in college, Hannon Hill, which still exists today. He then used his earnings from Hannon Hill to start Pardot. He bootstrapped Pardot with his earnings from Hannon Hill, recruited a small and scrappy team to build it, and eventually sold it to ExactTarget.

Poornima: "Hi David! Thanks for agreeing to chat with me today. I was thrilled to learn that a fellow Duke grad built a successful startup outside of Silicon Valley. Let's start with undergrad, because you mentioned that was when you started your first business. What were you doing at Duke?"

David: "I started college in 1998 and majored in Economics. I also built a lot of websites for researchers and sororities. I'd hand it to them, and then they'd say: *'I want to change it.'* This was before WordPress existed. So I figured they needed an easy-to-use content management system. I approached one of my professors for money to build the business over a summer. The business was Hannon Hill. I built it up to a 25-person company, and it's still doing great today."

Poornima: "That's awesome! So what happened next?"

David: "I studied the online marketing space. I noticed that there were businesses marketing directly to individuals [consumers, or B2C], but there weren't good solutions to market to other businesses [B2B]. They didn't have good tools for CRM, webinar management, etc. So I started with that thesis."

Poornima: "This is while you were running Hannon Hill?"

David: "Yes."

Poornima: "Got it. OK, so what did you do next?"

David: "In the first 45 days of Pardot, we decided to create a product to generate leads that did PPC [pay-per-click] arbitrage. We were going to buy ads against enterprise software terms, generate leads, and then sell them to vendors. Our goal was to pay $100 for a lead, then sell that lead for $50 to 5 vendors."

Poornima: "What happened when you showed it to customers?"

David: "We took our MVP [minimum viable product] to customers, and they actually thought the tool we created to generate these leads was more interesting. It did things like create landing pages, set up forms, and track leads. Basically, it was a tool to generate leads, and that's what they wanted. They wanted to do it themselves."

Poornima: "Who was your initial customer segment, and how did you reach out to your initial set of customers?"

David: "Our customers were tech companies, and we reached out to companies we were working with at Hannon Hill."

Poornima: "That's great, so you had a deep relationship with them that you could leverage. What happened after you decided to pivot?"

David: "Yeah, so this was March 1st of 2007. In April we decided to go in this new direction, and we worked on it until September 2007."

Poornima: "How did you go about building the product?"

David: "My co-founder, Adam Blitzer, focused on product management, marketing, and customer support. I built version 1.0 of Pardot in PHP, and the summer of 2007 we hired a bunch of interns from Georgia Tech as well as a lead engineer. We were funding it through Hannon Hill and used Hannon Hill as a test customer."

Poornima: "How did you scale your customer base?"

David: "We hired our first sales rep. We paid him $2500 monthly salary plus 15% commission for first-year sales."

Poornima: "What was his background?"

David: "He wasn't familiar with the space. He was selling enterprise back-office software. So we spent a lot of one-on-one time walking him through the product."

Poornima: "Wow, it's great that he was able to learn quickly and add value."

David: "Yeah, we were extremely lucky. When he started he was pretty entry-level, but he figured out the market and messaging. Within 2 years, he built out a sales team and went on to become our VP of sales."

Poornima: "So you had a pretty junior team: interns coding and an entry-level sales guy. Were you concerned at all about balancing the team's experience level?"

David: "We could only afford junior people, but we focused on hiring people for what their abilities could be."

Poornima: "That's great. So, let's switch gears and talk about the business. How did it grow over the 5 years that you were working on it?"

David: "We focused on generating recurring revenue combined with strong gross margins and strong renewal rates, and eventually that leads to strong predictability. In the first year we made $3K, the second year $485K, and the third year $1.25M. We focused on 5% growth per week, and then slowly lowered it over time. I wrote a post about it on my blog."[114]

Poornima: "Thanks, I'll check it out and offer it to readers; I think it would be extremely helpful for them. Now let's talk about the acquisition. How did that get started?"

David: "Back in June of 2012, ExactTarget was looking to partner with a marketing automation company. They knew they were strong in the B2C market but felt like they had missed the B2B. They originally approached Marketo for a partnership and put a program in place with them. They soon discovered that the organizations just weren't aligned culturally, but they did realize the B2B market was important."

Poornima: "It's interesting to see how culture and fit are important, even for a partnership. What happened next?"

David: "They approached us and asked for a demo. We didn't know if they were looking for a partner or looking to acquire us. We flew up to Indianapolis and shared everything. After the demo they kept asking us for more info. Then on August 15th [2012], they handed us a term sheet with an initial offer of $60M. We spent about 2 weeks negotiating, and eventually arrived at $95.5M plus some other stuff. In September we started due diligence, and by October 9th we closed the deal."

Poornima: "And since there were no investors, you and your co-founder basically benefited. Did you stay on?"

David: "I stayed for 0 days. I had no earn out. My co-founder stayed, and 8 months later ExactTarget was acquired by Salesforce."

Poornima: "That's awesome, and you had no outside investment, so it was a pretty sweet deal for you. What did you do next?"

David: "I started to look for a building to buy. I found a place with 100K square feet and closed the deal in December 2012. It's now Atlanta Tech Village[115] and houses 200 startups."

Poornima: "Great to hear that you're building a community in Atlanta, David! Any final takeaways for our readers?"

David: "Timing was super important. Marketing automation was already around, but B2B was really behind. Our competitors had been in the space for 5+ years, and they were fatigued by the time the market exploded in 2011. If we had done it earlier, the market wouldn't have been receptive."

Poornima: "It's also a great lesson in pursuing an idea even if there is competition! Let's briefly talk about your new startup, Kevy. How did you come up with the idea for it?"

David: "Kevy came out of Pardot. I noticed that for every 1 product you connect with, there are 10 more products customers want to connect. So I discovered that there was a need for a cloud middleware tool to connect products to each other."

Poornima: "There is definitely a need for that. Thanks a lot David for doing the interview, and I wish you a lot of success in your new venture!"

Just to recap, here's what we learned from David Cummings:

1. **You can leverage your learnings from one business to start another.** David began Hannon Hill[116], then soon discovered the need to generate business leads for it. That led him to build a tool to generate leads, which eventually became Pardot.

2. **Build something small and get it in front of customers.** Within 45 days, David had built the first version of Pardot. When he showed it to customers, they didn't want to buy leads; they wanted the tool that generated them. Based on customer feedback, he quickly pivoted and then spent 6 months building out the product.

3. **You don't need an experienced team.** Since David was right out of college and bootstrapping the business, he couldn't afford to hire experienced engineers and salespeople. He was fortunate to find a very talented entry-level sales guy and recruited engineering interns to build the product.

4. **You can build a sizable business without outside funding.** David went after enterprise customers and focused on generating recurring revenues early on. This helped him grow to a million-dollar business in 3 years.

5. **You can build a successful software company outside of Silicon Valley!** David built Pardot in Atlanta, GA, and the acquiring company, ExactTarget, was headquartered in Indianapolis, IN.

Epilogue

If you've gone through this whole book and done all the exercises, then kudos to you! You've done some substantial work, and should be proud of yourself for taking the steps needed to transform your idea into a software product.

Even if you've used this book to build a prototype, attract early adopters, and launch your product, I know deep down there may be some lingering feelings of uncertainty. You might be wondering: *"What's next?"*

Building software is an ongoing process.

If you launched and are seeing a lot of interest, then you'll need to take the time to scale your software infrastructure to meet the needs of your growing customer base. Those are more advanced topics, which I'll have to share in a future book!

However, if you launch and things are a little quiet, know that not all is lost. You'll need to continue to refine the product and educate customers about what you have to offer. Refining and educating is the work that people are often reluctant to do. But as you've seen from the interviews in the book, it's what many successful founders did to get to the next level.

I want your strongest takeaway from the book to be the following: building isn't enough; you also have to invest in generating demand and refining your product.

After I sent out my manuscript for peer review, my editor pointed out a post on Reddit[117] describing how companies like Airbnb, Dropbox, and even Reddit itself used some unconventional tactics to acquire their early adopters. The tactics listed in the post demonstrate that you have to keep trying new approaches to get the word out about your product.

Generating demand might take weeks, months, or years. It has definitely taken many companies that long—even those that might appear to be overnight successes! If you dig down deep in a founder's story, you're sure to discover a path of failures that came first.

Finally, this book was meant to be a way for us to connect, but it doesn't have to be the only way. Please feel free to reach out to me on Twitter @poornima. I'm looking forward to hearing how your ideas have transformed!

About the Author

Poornima Vijayashanker is currently the founder at Femgineer, an education startup that helps empower engineers, founders, and product leads to transform their ideas into tangible, high-impact products.

Poornima has also been a lecturer at Duke University's Pratt School of Engineering, an entrepreneur-in-residence at 500 Startups, and is currently the lead mentor-in-residence at Techstars in New York City.

She was the founding engineer at Mint.com, where she helped build, launch, and scale the product until its acquisition in 2009.

When she's not building products or companies she enjoys Bikram yoga, rock climbing, and running. Poornima lives in sunny Palo Alto, CA with her husband and two cats: Colby Jack and Riley.

REFERENCES

Introduction

1. http://femgineer.com/learn/lean-product-development/

2. http://500.co/

Chapter 1

3. https://www.codemontage.com/

4. http://startupweekend.org/

5. https://www.styleseat.com/

Chapter 2

6. http://femgineer.com/blog/

7. https://femgineer.com/learn/lean-product-development/

8. https://www.rescuetime.com/

9. http://www.boomeranggmail.com/hp3/index.html/

10. http://www.shopify.com/

11. http://www.crunchbase.com/organization/shopify/

Chapter 3

12. http://premoney.co/

13. http://500.co/

14. The term earlyvangelist was coined by Steve Blank in his book Four Steps to Epiphany

15. http://www.amazon.com/Positioning-The-Battle-Your-Mind-ebook/dp/B006B7LQ90

16. https://www.heroku.com/

17. https://www.rackspace.com/

18. https://www.engineyard.com/

Chapter 4

19. http://www.buvettegastrotheque.com/

20. http://www.ottopizzeria.com/

21. http://52weeksofux.com/post/385981879/you-are-not-your-user

22. http://femgineer.com/learn/lean-product-development/

23. http:/tweepi.com/

24. https://bufferapp.com/

25. http://www.bnbflow.com/

Chapter 5

26. http://lifehacker.com/

27. http://lifehacker.com/312083/is-mint-ready-for-your-money/

28. http://www.wufoo.com/

29. http://www.google.com/google-d-s/createforms.html/

30. https://docs.google.com/forms/d/11ZB4ff6H72ekAdUUye AYOiS7YdSiOMWVCComkkKQv0k/viewform

31. http://rosenfeldmedia.com/books/interviewing-users/

Chapter 6

32. http://en.wikipedia.org/wiki/Persona

Chapter 7

33. http://www.olark.com/

34. http:///www.meetup.com/femgineers/

35. http://en.wikipedia.org/wiki/Website_wireframe

36. https://www.youtube.com/watch?v=2UUIPIzVpGs&list=PL NZFyTfZybcz5WLC0wuk8MVfxSS984iT6&index=2

37. http://www.slideshare.net/poornimav/validate-your-mvp-on-paper

38. https://balsamiq.com

39. http://www.invisionapp.com/

40. http://mashable.com/2010/07/15/wireframing-tools/

Chapter 8

41. http://www.olark.com/

Chapter 9

42. http://femgineer.com/2012/08/how-to-keep-your-startup-engineer-sane/

43. http://www.pivotaltracker.com/

44. https://www.tindie.com/

45. http://www.crunchbase.com/organization/tindie/

Chapter 10

46. "Content marketing." Wikipedia.org. http://en.wikipedia.org/wiki/Content_marketing

47. http://blog.mailchimp.com/how-asthmatic-kitty-is-using-email-to-redefine-street-teams/

48. http://blog.gumroad.com/post/88581663698/google-analytics-campaign-tracking

49. http://moz.com/blog/how-to-perform-the-worlds-greatest-seo-audit

50. http://moz.com/researchtools/ose

51. http://femgineer.com/2014/03/journey-from-founding-engineer-to-founder-being-honest-about-what-you-donthave/

52. http://femgineer.com/2014/03/founders-is-your-head-filled-with-questions/

53. http://nathanbarry.com/samuel-hulick-37000-self-published-book/

54. https://www.airbnb.com/stories

55. http://bizeebee.com/2012/10/victoria-klein-yoga

56. http://launchrock.co/

57. http://unbounce.com/

58. http://istockphoto.com/

59. http://mailchimp.com/

60. http://kb.mailchimp.com/article/how-do-i-build-and-design-my-signup-form-and-response-emails/

61. https://convertkit.com/

62. https://mixpanel.com/

Chapter 12

63. Croll, Alistair and Benjamin Yoskovitz. Lean Analytics. Sebastopol, CA: O'Reilly, 2013.

---

64. Croll, Alistair and Benjamin Yoskovitz. Lean Analytics. Sebastopol, CA: O'Reilly, 2013.

65. https://www.dropbox.com

66. https://www.hellosign.com/

67. https://www.airbnb.com/

68. http://www.mobissimo.com/search_airfare.php

69. http://www.kissmetrics.com

70. http://www.mixpanel.com

71. Margin is revenue minus the expenses to create and sell the product.

72. www.google.com/analytics/

73. "Set up the web tracking code." Google.com. https://support.google.com/analytics/answer/1008080

74. http://try.framed.io/

75. "Framed Data." Crunchbase.com. http://www.crunchbase.com/organization/framed-data

Chapter 13

76. "HTTP Secure." Wikipedia.org. http://en.wikipedia.org/wiki/HTTP_Secure

77. "Best Practices for Using Cookies." Truste.com. http://www.truste.com/blog/2011/12/02/best-practices-for-using-cookies/

78. https://stripe.com/

79. https://www.balancedpayments.com/

80. http://www.business.ftc.gov/documents/bus61-can-spam-act-compliance-guide-business/

81. http://www.truste.com/

82. http://www.verisign.com/

83. https://loader.io/

84. http://loadimpact.com/

85. http://www.browserstack.com/

86. http://www.olark.com

87. https://getsatisfaction.com/corp/

88. https://www.helpscout.net/

89. https://www.uservoice.com/

90. http://www.zendesk.com/

91. https://www.statuspage.io/

92. http://newrelic.com/

93. http://www.pressfriendly.com/

94. Ries, Eric. The Lean Startup: How Today's Entrepreneurs Use Continuous Innovation to Create Radically Successful Businesses. New York: Crown Business, 2011.

95. http://www.hipcamp.com/

96. http://www.crunchbase.com/organization/hipcamp

Chapter 14

97. http://www.sandler.com/

98. http://theyogipreneur.com/

99. https://www.kickstarter.com/

100. https://www.indiegogo.com/

101. https://fundly.com/

102. http://angelpad.org/

103. http://500.co/

104. http://www.techstars.com/

105. http://www.ycombinator.com/

106. http://avc.com/

107. http://www.bhorowitz.com/

108. http://blog.semilshah.com/

109. http://venturehacks.com/

110. http://www.angel.com/

111. http://www.pardot.com/

112. http://kevy.com/

113. http://.atlantaventures.com/

114. http://davidcummings.org/2014/07/22/recurring-revenue-and-week-over-week-growth/

115. http://atlantatechvillage.com/

116. http://www.hannonhill.com/

Epilogue

117. "How startups such as Dropbox, Airbnb, Groupon and others acquired their first users." Reddit.com. http://www.reddit.com/r/Entrepreneur/comments/2clqa3/how_startups_such_as_dropbox_airbnb_groupon_and/

Made in the USA
Lexington, KY
27 April 2018